Winning Through Career Change

Six steps to navigate your way to a brighter future

Steve Preston
The Career Catalyst®

Printed and bound in Great Britain by
CPI Group (UK) Ltd, Croydon, CR0 4YY

ISBN 978-0-9571292-3-8

Dedications

This book is dedicated to:

Sue Blake - For your inspiration, wisdom and belief in me to become a published author of a series of career and personal development books that will change lives. You are sadly missed but your light still shines on us.

Don Presland - Best mate, beer buddy, colleague and 'Ace of Spades' portfolio careerist. Your 'magic' lives on.

PRAISE

About The Book

"Changing jobs for any reason can be the great turning point in your career and life. This excellent book shows you how to make the rest of your work life the best of your work life."

Brian Tracy – Internationally renowned American Author, Motivational Speaker, leading authority on the development of human potential

"Career Change! Just the very words fill so many people with fear and doubt. Those worries can now be phrased in the past tense. With Steve Preston's excellent new book: Winning Through Career Change - anyone can take control of their lives, their results, and their future.

Dive into the Cycle Model and discover just how much you have to offer. Take a fresh P.E.R.S.P.E.C.T.I.V.E. on everything in your life. Realise you are never too old to change and how you can now enjoy the rest of your working life.

Steve's down to earth, clearly defined, practical ideas are just what anyone considering changing careers is looking for. It's your guide to the future, a road map to new successes, and a friend always by your side. Read on - you'll be so pleased you did."

Peter Thomson - The UK's Most Prolific Information Product Creator

"Steve's book is 'The Knowledge' of how to turn your career change into a challenging yet positive and uplifting life changing experience. A must have guide for anyone embarking on a new voyage of career discovery!"

Gail Gibson (UK)

"This book will be read by people, who like me, find themselves at the crossroads of their working life. It will especially appeal to people who want to change career because of a lack of fulfilment in what they are doing to earn a living.

It is often a huge step to seek help and then once that step is taken, to find the right advice to help move you forward on a 'voyage of self-discovery'. This book becomes your friend and your mentor as you take stock of your life and look at how you can reinvent yourself as you 'navigate your way to a brighter future'.

As you read through each step prescribed by Steve, you will soon feel relaxed as you realise that he is talking to you and you alone. The style of the writing makes you feel as though you are having a one on one session with Steve himself! At each stage of the book you are challenged to think about where you are in your life and where you want to be. It invites you to re-evaluate your priorities. It questions your thinking and makes you step outside your comfort zone. All this is done in a way that is not intrusive or threatening. It makes you feel good about what you need to do to change your career.

You have reached out your hand and asked for help and Steve has responded in a compassionate, caring way that makes you sit up and take notice and then actually take the next step towards 'becoming the architect of your own future."

Ewen Anderson (Australia)

"As someone keen to make a career change this book has been a revelation for me, providing me with a process and a path to start my journey. Prior to reading this book I felt I was heading into the abyss, but after reading Winning Through Career Change I now feel I am boarding a train for an exciting destination and I'm actually looking forward to the journey too!

The book had me engaged from the first chapter, so much so I missed my bus stop on the way to work! It's a very engaging and inspiring read, with case studies reinforcing how change is possible. As I read through the chapters I was anticipating the point you reach in so many books, where the material 'dries up' and it all becomes a little obvious and open ended. Not so, with this book, as I got to the end without ever getting that sinking feeling.

If you are considering change and want to make the change in a structured way, this is the book for you. I was so inspired, I started my journey straight away and am now working with Steve for additional support through the process; after all train journeys are far more fun with a companion!"

Sandie Harries (UK)

"Winning Through Career Change is the most inspiring personal development book I have read in years. The author sets a very logical path to follow. One that is difficult to see while stuck doing another job. For me, the book was liberating. I would suggest reading it in its entirety then going back and doing the exercises in order. A must buy book for anyone considering a career change. Thank you Steve Preston!"

Serial Entrepreneur (Canada)

"If you are serious about finding something in life that you love to do and doing it, look no further than this book. Whether you have got stuck in a career rut or just feel it is time for change, these six steps will show you the way. In the introduction, the author, Steve Preston, talks about 'The Power of Passion', and his passion for helping you discover your true marketability, and navigate your way to a brighter future shines out on every page. What really makes this book stand out is the emphasis on doing the inner work before embarking on the practical aspects of career change. With its blend of essential information, tried and tested steps and exercises and inspiring case studies, (such as the one about the chap with a true portfolio career, which includes being a magician!), you know you are in experienced hands. This is an empowering read in every sense of the word."

Leda Sammarco (UK)

"I purchased this book because I was at a transition point in my career and also opted to complete Steve's Online Career Change Programme. The book together with the programme were really helpful. The exercises were easy-to-follow and I found them really useful to focus my thinking and define what I wanted to do next. They got me to think about aspects of my career that I would not have considered by myself.

The case studies in the book were interesting and very easy to relate to also. The 6 Step Career Navigation Cycle process described in the book is a simple concept but is thorough, thought-provoking and affirming. Knowing that I have fully considered my career and life choices thanks to the book has given me reassurance and confidence in the decisions I have made since. I highly recommend Winning Through Career Change to anyone at a career crossroads."

Jim Enright (Ireland)

"I wish I had read this book ten years ago when I was questioning my career and my life. I love how Steve demystifies the process and emotions that people go through when making a career change and offers clear practical steps, help and guidance. This is a book about how to take your life in your hands and follow your heart. Thank you Steve!"

Tara W Cox (Australia)

"I'm wondering if you're saying to yourself "Not another one of those 'self-help' books" ...and you'd be right! ...it's NOT another one of those self-help books. This one takes quite a different slant and focuses the attention of those people who have become 'lost in their jobs' and need some help to move forward to change careers. Therefore the issue isn't whether or not to read Winning Through Career Change, it is whether you can afford not to, as Steve Preston's Career Navigation Cycle is a proven process that leads people from darkness to light... and I should know.

Steve's 'Career Navigation Cycle' is a lifeline that sits at the core of his coaching programmes and book and this presented me with a rational, systematic process to follow, when working through my own career change. The topsy-turvy 'roller coaster' journey allowed me to 'let go' of the past and regain confidence whilst building a sense of realisation and liberation that I could pursue something I truly enjoyed and life became much brighter and exciting filled with possibilities. The easy style of the book reads as if you're having a chat with a friend who is keen to give advice and stimulus to move you forward to achieve your true potential. Steve's wealth of experience and passion will positively propel you, like me, to a new era that you may not have thought possible."

Steve Engwell (UK)

"Once again job seekers can depend on Steve Preston to shine a bright light to illuminate the murky path for those in career-change mode. 'Winning Through Career Change' is an invaluable missive for all job seekers on either side of the Atlantic and beyond. As a practicing Career Counselor, it is important for me to recognize the effort Steve and others put forth to help the job seeking public."

Al Smith (USA)

"Winning Through Career Change is just like its author Steve Preston – a winner! Steve has done an outstanding job helping other people navigate the exciting, yet challenging and turbulent, 21st century work environment. Steve clearly lets the reader know they must take personal responsibility for their professional satisfaction. His refreshing advice and easy to follow 6 step process provides the healing and hope so many people who are changing careers desperately need. The carefully selected quotes included are also inspiring. This is a read which will pay for itself dozens of times over!"

Brother Gregory Cellini, O.S.F – Host, Thank God For Monday Radio Show, New York (USA)

PRAISE

for Steve's Career Coaching Work

"Steve is expert in unlocking potential and helping clients make an impact. His coaching methods and materials are thought provoking, engaging and deliver results."

Dean Creamer, OBE

"I would describe Steve as the 'Anthony Robbins' of Career Development. This man takes any negative thinking and re-frames it as positive outlook. Put bluntly I was lucky enough to be on one of Steve's workshops and before I met him 'I couldn't get arrested'. Two weeks after his course I had over 3 job offers from stock brokerages. There should be more people in this country like Mr Preston and you can take that to the bank!!!!"

Liam Byrne

"Steve's knowledge and understanding of the science of work and career is exemplary. His ability to see how to help others to realign their internal belief systems with their need to work produces explosive results. This helps you to attain new goals and create new work pathways that had not previously been considered available or possible before. His Breakthrough Career Change Programme is inspiring,

creative and an essential rewiring for the brain of somebody at a dead end."

Simon Dwight

"Steve is one of the UK's market leaders in Career and Personal Development. He is incredibly skilled in unlocking and opening your mind to believing in and fulfilling your own true potential". Steve is in demand; work with him while you can!

Debbie Smith

"I engaged Steve's support during my transition to independence, following many years of working within the corporate environment. It was a key point in my life where I needed to stop and reflect upon what my future held. Steve along with his associates coached me through a number of key areas in order for me to confidently pursue my personal goal and the process of re-branding myself as 'ME'. The power of coaching is not fully understood until you have experienced it firsthand. With Steve's extensive knowledge and a never ending 'toolkit', it makes the process not only enjoyable but an empowering one that I can fully recommend."

Jane Seeley

"I've worked with Steve and his team at SMP Solutions for a number of years and cannot express enough how supportive they've been in helping with my personal career development over the years. Through their support I've transitioned from a manager of a technical support department at a college to running my own businesses and finally getting a good work-life balance. The coaching, guidance and support has been (and still is) truly invaluable as I continue to personally develop and as my companies grow!"

Lee Dredge

"At a time when I felt at the peak of a career crossroads, Steve not only focused my mind but helped me to understand what it was that I really wanted and needed. Steve not only gave me a sense of direction but opened my mind to the situation I was in and where my future lay, in terms of career progression but also the need I felt for a position that had meaning and that could give me a sense of achievement that reached beyond the 9-5. Steve gave me some great advice on building my CV and helped me to fine tune the highlights and achievements I wanted to present to prospective employers. After spending months deliberating, within weeks I had two offers on the table from two fantastic companies and had the luxury of choosing which offer to accept! My career has really taken off but without Steve's help I believe I would still be confused and unsure of where to begin, so I could not make a higher recommendation!"

Sasha Harbridge

"Working with Steve on his Executive Breakthrough Career Development Programme is best described as the difference between looking at a road map and having a GPS in my car!

I would never dream of heading towards an unknown destination without one or other but quite simply, Steve's Executive Coaching Programme has helped me keep on track in my career change journey. Despite the diversions and road blocks which most of us encounter when visiting previously uncharted territory of changing career path, I do not believe that I could have got in the driving seat let alone stayed the course without his support!

Working with Steve has helped me focus on my ultimate destination and enabled me to be in the driving seat of my chosen career path. Until I started the programme, I was blinded by the oncoming headlights and stuck in a jam. Steve's Career Navigation Cycle process and coaching enabled me to set off and successfully change direction without losing sight of where I ultimately wanted to be.

I would also recommend 'Winning Though Career Change' as an absolute must read and having Steve as your navigator on the most exciting journey you will ever make!"

Bill Stewart

"I found coaching with Steve hugely valuable and inspiring. Steve helped me to recognise my skills and attributes, and helped me to see that I have a unique contribution and value and guided me towards achieving the career of my dreams. I particularly valued his individual approach whereby he went at my pace and the sessions were tailored to my needs as an individual. He motivated me to succeed by helping me set powerful goals and I am now well on my way to having a successful portfolio career. I recommend Steve as a Career Coach very highly"

Bridget Morris

"I was introduced to Steve at a time when I was considering my future career options. Steve brought a wealth of experience, tools and insight to help me understand myself better and how I could approach my career, job searches and interviews. He was an integral part of my transitioning successfully to a new role."

Adam Thomas

"Working with Steve has made a real and lasting difference to my life - sounds dramatic but it's true. His way of working really resonated with me; we had fun but got through a whole load of difficult stuff! Steve helped me to find a good work-life balance, to recognise what I had to offer and to have the confidence to demonstrate it to others. As a result, I am more focused at work, achieving great results that others are

recognising and happier at home. Steve has continued to be a confidante and friend to me and I am so pleased to have met him."

Lisa Hughes

"When I was stuck in a rut and looking to develop my career to the next stage, I enlisted Steve's help to provide the focus and clarity I needed to ensure that I was applying for the right jobs and to also market myself in the most effective way. Steve helped me to really understand my true marketability, what was important to me in my next role and motivated me to achieve job success. He is encouraging, professional and expert and I highly recommend him for any professionals and executives looking to develop their career."

Richard Castleton

Acknowledgements

I wish to thank some very special people who have helped turn my vision into reality to achieve my goal of becoming a published author of a series of career and personal development books which will make a difference to the lives of others:

Ed Peppitt, my original publisher, now project manager, for your continued support, guidance and encouragement in making this paperback version possible.

Steve Engwell, client now friend and colleague, for your all-round brilliant support and remarkable copy-editing. I feel privileged to have supported you to win through your career change and helped unlock your latent creativity and natural talents to take you 'from the darkness and into the light' to become a shining star!

Tara Winona, my amazing Illustrator, for bringing my book to life with your vision, passion, vibrancy, energy and incredible art. Isn't it fantastic that my book projects have helped you unlock your true potential and fulfill your talent by sharing your creative, artistic genius with the world? You have truly arrived!

Santosh Sagoo, for giving me the opportunity to support you to win through your career change and in return providing me with invaluable feedback, insight, encouragement and motivation to make this book possible. You are a real 'Angel'.

Debbie Smith, for your encouragement, belief and friendship, sharing in many successes and for kindly providing material on Personal Branding.

Gail Gibson, for your inspiration, support, friendship, and input for Portfolio Careers, Networking and Social Media.

Steve Bridger for kindly providing information and inspiration for the self-employed career options from your excellent 'Success Before Start-up' book and workshop.

Rob McCargow, for kindly introducing some wonderful clients and providing content for Interim Management.

Brian Tracy, a brilliant speaker, author and psychologist and a source of constant inspiration.

Peter Thomson, business guru and 'Product Creation genius'. Your workshops inspired me to stretch and create products that will make a difference to the lives and careers of others.

To my wonderful wife, Lin, for your love, patience, encouragement, unbending support and being my sounding board and rock, on yet another book project.

To all my clients and contacts who have agreed to be featured in the various case studies in real name or pseudonyms to protect your identities. You are testimony to what amazing career changes can be achieved with the right mindset, belief and positive actions.

CONTENTS

INTRODUCTION

Can you imagine how would it feel to wake up each Monday morning in the knowledge that you have an exciting and enjoyable week ahead, doing work you love? Wouldn't that be just great?

The sobering statistics are that research consistently shows 1 in 2 people is in the 'wrong job' and 2 out of 3 are unfulfilled in their jobs. Therefore millions of people are unhappy and in the 'wrong job' or career. We all know people like this, don't we? They are forever bemoaning their lot but never do anything about it or just accept that this is the way is has to be, as after all you don't have to enjoy your job, do you? **Or do you?!**

Maybe you recognise these feelings? The reality is that only a small percentage of people ever take the 'leap of faith' and decide to take positive action to make a career change. You will want to join this special 'club', wont' you?

I will show you throughout the book ***how you can change your thinking so you learn that you do have CHOICE and how to take control of your career and life, not just now but for the rest of your working life and just think how good that will be***.

By reading this book you will transform your life if you are looking to change career. You will feel energized; develop a real sense of purpose and focus. People I work with tell me *'that the clouds will lift'* giving you clarity, self-awareness and a target to aim for. You will be much better equipped to know what is important to you in your life and career moving forward, understand what you have to offer an employer or what you can offer as a business owner, to sell yourself effectively and above all know what it takes to make a successful career change or transition. Once you have developed this inner self-awareness you will be in a good position to take the learning and knowledge you have gained into your new career, whatever you decide to do.

I will be sharing some of my own career change journey. Many of my learning points, as well as some interesting and inspiring case studies, will show you how you can win through career change to *navigate your way to a brighter future* and redesign an exciting new career!

Each Chapter relates to a step of my Career Navigation Cycle and has specific exercises and tools which are all part of the process to help you achieve a successful outcome. My aim is to inspire you to get started on your voyage of self-discovery and ultimately 'take the leap of faith' to find the new fulfilling career or work for you.

To help you cross the finishing line and win through, I will be providing some 'Winning Steers' and also 'Pit Stops', to encourage you to take time out and momentarily stop and absorb what you have just read and 'refuel' by considering some of the comments or advice before moving on. 'Pit Stops' are a necessary part of the strategy to win through.

Isn't it reassuring to know that, you like me and the many case studies featured, will also come to *'love Mondays'*, enjoy the work you do and achieve a fulfilling life?

How Do You Feel About Your Career? - Have You Reached A Career Crossroads?

'Career' is defined by the Oxford English Dictionary "as a person's course or progress through life (or a distinct portion of life)". In this definition career is understood to relate to a range of aspects of an individual's life, learning and work. You may not have previously thought about this **but your career and life are inextricably linked.** Why?... *Because if you are happy in your job or career, this has a direct impact on how you feel about life in general.* Likewise if you are unhappy in your life, this is bound to affect your performance in your job or career.

To help you start your voyage of self-discovery you should complete the *Current Situation Quiz*. This will set the scene and allow you to put your first stake in the ground to highlight **why** you feel you want to change career. Being totally honest, as you must be with all the exercises in this book, consider the following statements and put Y (yes) or N (no) as applicable to you after each statement or a separate document or piece of paper.

You can also find a downloadable electronic version of this quiz in the bonus extras on my Career Catalyst website www.steveprestonthecareercatalyst.com

Current Situation Quiz

1. I don't know where my career is heading and feel lost
2. I've been in the same job or industry for years and feel stuck in a rut, unfulfilled
3. I am not achieving / aware of my true potential or purpose
4. I no longer look forward to going to work each day
5. I may have the opportunity for voluntary redundancy but am not sure whether I should pursue this
6. As part of an organisational restructure, my job will disappear. I feel apprehensive as I have been identified to be redeployed into a completely different role, moving away from my specialism
7. I would like to find work that is fulfilling but I'm afraid of trying something new

8. I want to make a career change but have no idea what to do next
9. I want to make a career change but have so many ideas I can't decide what I should do
10. I am returning to work following a career break/ redundancy and seeking a new career/life path
11. I would like to start my own business/be my own boss, but don't know what to do, whether I am capable of making it work or where to begin
12. I am getting interviews but no job offers so feel like giving up
13. I dread applying for new jobs
14. I spend too much time working or commuting and wish to redress my work-life balance

Why Do You Want To Change?

I would hazard a guess that you have at least three Yes's, haven't you? You may even have most of them. There are no right or wrong answers but whatever your number, each 'yes' you have selected shows that you are at a career crossroads and is a reason **why** you need to read this book and work through my Six Step Career Navigation Cycle process so you can win through your career change!

If you have several Yes's, then you have either just reached a career crossroads, have done so for a while and not addressed your situation or maybe you have been in denial about your situation? Either way you will definitely get real value from this book, so read on. You also have the reassurance of knowing that I will help you to rethink and redesign your career and life path to find fulfilment in your work and life, just as I did over a decade ago.

My mantra is:

"You spend more waking hours at work than in any other activity. Life is too short so why be unhappy? Take 'the leap of faith' and do what you love!"

As you read on I will help you stay positive and proactive whilst also discovering how to avoid some of the pitfalls I made during my career change and have seen many other people make since. Regardless of how you currently feel about your career, you can be assured that this book will help you navigate the 'career transition maze' in a more focused and confident way, with a proven process to follow to achieve your desired outcomes. If you are unable to see this far ahead, don't worry as I will guide you through the career change process to help you create a new vision for your success.

What Started My Change Journey?

In 2001, I was at a career crossroads, facing redundancy, as my company was relocating. I saw this as a positive opportunity as deep down I knew that I wanted to change career. I had become 'an expert' in my profession but I was bored and my job wasn't giving me the buzz I was looking for. It was time to move on and do something different.

Although I saw changing career as a positive I couldn't see past the 'fog'. I was excited about the future but didn't know what it looked like or how to get there! Likewise, if you are currently going through career transition or looking to make a career change you may also feel excited but apprehensive or simply uncertain and lost about what to do next and how to move forward.

Equally, you might be 'gung ho' and full of drive and determination to make your career change or you are lacking confidence, motivation and self-belief to make a successful career change, even though you want to. Don't worry as these are all natural responses and you are not alone. I can assure you that there are many other people in exactly your situation and you, unlike many others, at least have the benefit of reading and taking the learning from this book to show you the six key steps to make a successful career change and end up doing work you love.

I'm sure you will have had some career and life defining moments in your time. One of the most significant for me was when I realised *I didn't want somebody telling me what job I should be doing, where I should live and work and feel I was beholden to any company for my future.* I wanted to be in control of my life and career, what I now call 'being the architect of your own future'. So, it was my choice to opt for redundancy, look to change career and 'let go' of my past. You will come to realise by reading this book that we all have CHOICE but also things to 'let go' of.

Little did I know that the resulting journey would have such a profound impact on my life. In my process of self-discovery I developed new passions for career and personal development, which helped take my career in a completely different direction. It would have been inconceivable that I would ultimately become MD of my specialist Career and People Development Consultancy and also have my own personal brand as Steve Preston The Career Catalyst, top Career Coach, developer of inspirational career and personal development products, keynote speaker and an internationally acclaimed published author. I am forever **grateful** that I was bold and made the right choice, to become the architect of my own future. By doing so, I managed to successfully change careers to find work that I love and lead a fulfilling life, just as you can too.

What I now realise is that, as you will see consistently throughout this book, I have proven that you can always learn new skills. Moreover, by becoming self-aware, understanding what is important to you in your career and life and why and who you are and what you have to offer, you can change your perspective and reinvent yourself to open up new opportunities. I didn't see it this way when going through my career change and this might also be the case with you.

Likewise, you would not believe the number of new clients who lament the fact that they are *'just a generalist'*. Although they have actually done many different roles within their organisations, the paradox is that they feel they are disadvantaged, because it is hard to put them into an obvious 'box'. In my experience, it is a rare person who does realise the true value of having developed his or her career by working in a multitude of different functions and business disciplines, albeit in the same organisation. What if your mindset shifted to thinking and believing that, by having a wide range of skills, being flexible and adaptable and embracing change, this would put you in good stead for many different types of jobs?

In this book we will explore making a career change into a completely different type of employed job, numerous options for self-employment and starting a business of your own in the 21stcentury digital age and also touch on changing your career within your existing organisation. Put this way, does changing careers suddenly now look infinitely more achievable? I'm sure it does, so read on!

Having decided I wanted to change career, I faced a major dilemma, which you may well do also i.e. what was the best option to take?

Look for another senior management employed role but doing something completely different

OR

Set up my own business and be my own boss?

Being my own boss was definitely appealing, but there were some key questions to be answered i.e. what would I be the boss of? What would my business do? I had a number of ideas but nothing concrete. The kudos of a corporate executive position and the company benefits associated with it were equally attractive, but my dislike of company politics and time away from the family at constant (and often unnecessary) meetings was not!

How could I make my decision? If only I had a process to work through to help me. You may be feeling the same. The good news is this book has been specifically written with you in mind to take you on a voyage of self-discovery with a proven process to guide you to make an effective decision.

How Did I End Up Doing What I Do Now?

I get asked this question all the time. I suppose in a way it was a mixture of fate, accident and the Law of Attraction, which we will be revisiting at various points in the book. I cannot stress enough the importance and value of conducting your own research in shaping your career (more of this will follow, especially in Chapter 4) as this provided me with a breakthrough opportunity. I discovered a government sponsored programme that supported unemployed executives and professionals back to work. Run by an independent training and development company, I attended career development workshops and had 1:1 support a couple of days a week over a number of weeks.

I felt reassured that I was not alone and it made me realise the importance of a support network, something that I cannot stress strongly enough when looking to change career. We will revisit this in Chapter 1 and again cover networking in more detail in Chapter 4.

I will allude to the importance and impact of mindset in Chapter 1 and throughout the book, as I have learnt how important this is in making a successful career change. Unlike myself, many others on the course missed a real opportunity to try something different. Instead, they were dead set on doing 'more of the same', even if it was evident that such jobs were a thing of the past or they were too highly paid for the current market. They stubbornly stayed in their comfort zones, rather than facing their fears and exploring new opportunities. While they floundered others, like me, moved forward and made great progress changing careers, as you can too!

I found some of the key benefits from career coaching and career and personal development quickly renewed my energy, enthusiasm and confidence. The clouds started to lift; I could start to see things more clearly and was finding a new lease of life and sense of purpose. Although the course was good, I could see ways in which it could be improved, as I was really feeling in tune with the career development work. This created a sense of excitement by being able to make a positive contribution, as I could see a potential opportunity to utilise my previous management and people development skills. With my confidence renewed, I offered the MD of the training consultancy some constructive suggestions to improve the programme. I could see by changing the tone from teaching to adopting a more facilitative and coaching approach, it would make the course much more engaging and interactive, which I firmly believe is really important to aid learning.

One of the most enlightening learning points for me was the concept of the 'portfolio career'. This is a massive mindset shift from having a job to instead earning income from different business strands, skills and ideally interests and passions. This was really appealing and we will cover this in more depth in later Chapters of the book. The portfolio career concept has helped to transform my life, as well as that of many of my clients and other people I have met. I do much writing and speaking on portfolio careers. My 3rd book *'Portfolio Careers – How to Work for Passion, Pleasure & Profit'* has gained international recognition and positioned me as a global thought leader on the subject.

Although it may not seem to be the case to you right now, I learnt that you do have CHOICE and I know that when you also come to this realisation, you will have reached a key turning point in your career change!

I now had the motivation and self-belief to set up my own business, although I was still not clear what that business was going to look like. However, I did have some consultancy work already lined up in the Reward and Benefits arena and was keen to develop a portfolio career utilising skills I had developed over many years, a range of business interests including embracing my new passion for Career Development. Most importantly I was determined to take action and make it happen and you will see this is key to Chapter 6.

I finished the programme on the first anniversary of my late father's birthday with an absolute commitment to set up as self-employed, so that I would never forget the day. I dedicated my business, now SMP Solutions (Career & People Development) Ltd in his honour. As they say, the rest is history!

The MD of the training company asked me to make a cameo appearance at the next executive course to share with the group why I had chosen to set up my own business. As a result of the positive feedback from this first venture, I was invited to run a half day workshop. I then graduated to training a variety of full day workshops and providing 1:1 career advice and guidance support. In addition, I took another massive leap of faith by volunteering my services (albeit partly paid) to help the consultancy rewrite the whole career development programme. This paid back big time as things evolved further with me becoming their lead trainer and career coach in four locations whilst also helping to mentor and train new trainers. I was*becoming the architect of my own future*. With the help of this book, you can become the architect of your own wonderful new future too!

The Power Of Passion

My new journey had well and truly begun and it was both exciting and scary, nonetheless, I was determined that I was never going to look back. What became apparent was that the **more passionate I felt about the work I was doing, the more the work started coming my way**. The power of this cannot be underestimated, as channeled in the right way, passions can drive £'s or $'s! We will be exploring some 'Universal Laws of Success and Achievement' in more detail in Chapter 5.

Since achieving my own successful career transition, I have devoted the last dozen or more years of my life to becoming an expert in the field of Career Change, Career Transition, Career and Personal Development. I am more passionate than ever about making a difference and helping people win through their own career changes. How do I do this? By coaching you through a process which will give you the all the tools to make a successful change. Although this might be a difficult and challenging time of your life, wouldn't it be great to realise you are never too young or too old to make a successful career change to end up doing work you love and lead a fulfilling life? That would be really empowering and liberating, wouldn't it?

People tell me that my passion becomes infectious, which is why so much of my business comes from recommendations and referrals as wouldn't you want to work with someone who shows real enthusiasm, commitment, interest and passion for what they do? I will be constantly referring to the power of passion throughout this book. If you have never thought it possible that you **can** do work that you love, I would like to plant this seed with you now. *Why?* Because almost anything is possible with the right mindset, belief and positive actions!

Navigate Your Way To Success

Having achieved a successful career change myself and having seen what worked and what didn't, I was determined to make it easier for other people to make a winning career change. I also wanted to make sure that it would be easier regardless of their situation, length of career or level they had worked at. Since then I've worked with thousands of clients and established the common themes for successful career transition and change. When I analysed these and considered my own journey, **I discovered that there is a definite process to achieve a successful change**. With this in mind, I developed the 'SMP Career Navigation Cycle' which will be referred to henceforth as 'The Career Navigation Cycle', or 'the Cycle', which has proven to be a great success for thousands of people in a variety of situations, over many years.

The Cycle works in almost every conceivable situation providing you have had a reasonable career with at least a few years of paid employment. Evidence shows it is much easier for people to become derailed without such a practical structure and process to work through to keep you focused and on track. Therefore my Cycle will be a great benefit for you, as you work through your change.

You are likely to have some unfulfilled life goals. One of mine was to write books that will have a positive impact on people and make a difference to their lives. My first book was the internationally acclaimed *'Winning Through Redundancy'*. Although this was focused on redundancy, it was still a book about how to successfully manage and change your career and life, as the process is exactly the same. Such was the positive feedback that I was encouraged by readers, clients and my publisher, to create a revised version of the book solely focused on winning through career change. Now as a published author of a series of books and audio books, this is yet another opportunity for me to positively influence you by taking you through each step of my Cycle, Chapter by Chapter, helping you to reach a successful conclusion to *win through career change, navigate your way to a brighter future* and most importantly end up doing work you love.

Career Navigation Cycle

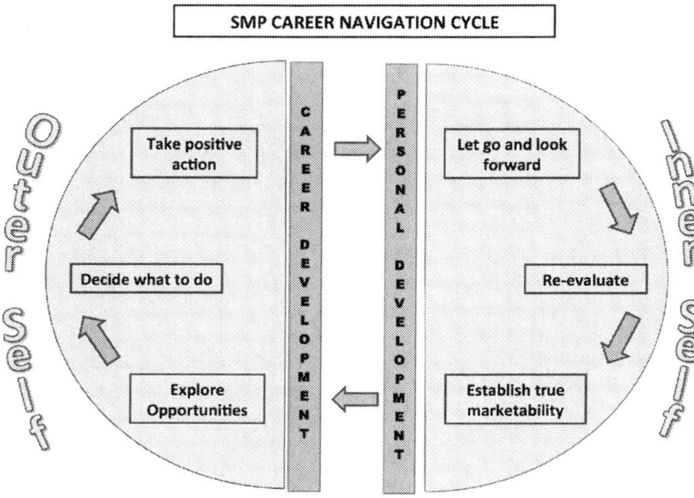

Career Navigation Cycle Overview of Each Step

Step 1 – Let go and look forward

You are what you think and feel. To tackle any major change you have to change your thinking – you have to learn to look forward not back

Step 2 – Re-evaluate

What is important to you in your career and life and WHY?

Step 3 – Establish your true marketability

Know who you are and what you have to offer – your 'complete package'

Step 4 – Explore Opportunities

Research, network, find and evaluate new opportunities

Step 5 – Decide what to do

Follow your passions; know what you want and where to find it

Step 6 – Take positive action

The future may look scary or exciting. Either way you must follow through with your career action plan to succeed!

My aim is purposefully very different to many other career books. My approach is to combine the power of Personal Development with practical Career Development strategies to unlock your true potential and help you fulfil your talent, whilst also helping you combat the psychological and emotional responses often associated with changing careers. My Cycle and Six Step process are aimed at keeping you on track and committed to taking your 'leap of faith' and winning through your career change to do work you love.

Steps 1-3 of the Cycle are integral to your ultimate success, because this is where the hard graft and real inner self, soul-searching work that most people rarely do, takes place. By putting in the effort in these Chapters you will be well positioned to set yourself up for a fulfilling career and life, providing you then continue to build momentum working through the rest of the Chapters and Steps of the Cycle. The final Chapters, Steps 4-6 of the Cycle are outer self work and contain much more in the way of practical career development activities, practical tips and case studies to help you complete the Cycle and achieve a successful outcome.

It is important to follow through each step of the Cycle, not skipping any of it, as there is a logical sequence to the process. You need to go through this Cycle, follow it right round and then you will come through the 'other side' having learnt a huge amount about yourself.

The process is like anything in life i.e. you have to put in the effort to get the reward. *There is no magic wand, there is no holy grail*, so you have to put in the effort to reap the return. You reap what you sow as the saying goes. There will inevitably be crossover along the way, so you might move back and forth between Steps but always with the next Step in mind.

Likewise the Cycle is also continuous as once you have successfully achieved your career change, it is very possible that you may well start the process again in a number of years' time as you grow and develop personally and professionally. You may also complete the Cycle and feel you need to start over again, as new things emerge, especially where you might need to let go or re-evaluate.

People say that having completed Step 6 and then moving back to Step 1 is like having created a bridge, which you can now easily cross to start navigating again. Only, this time you have a tried and tested Career Navigation Cycle process to follow with the confidence it worked first time round, so you can kick start things much more quickly on subsequent revisits.

Having established this is the right book for you, you are now ready to start work on your career change and turn your career into a brave new world of opportunity. The process is very individual, depending on your circumstances. There is no set timescale. For some people it can be days to work your way round, for others, weeks and some (including me) it was months. However, I did not have the benefit of the insights which you will have by reading this book. You may already realise that the impact of your career change journey can be an emotional roller coaster ride, but I will make sure it also becomes a great voyage of self-discovery for you.

Fasten your seatbelt and enjoy the journey!

CHAPTER 1

Let Go And Look Forward – Step 1

"Your past does not equal nor does it dictate your future... Focus on where you want to go, not what you fear"

Anthony Robbins, Entrepreneur, Author & Peak Performance Strategist

So, you are now aware that you are at a career crossroads and starting on a voyage of self-discovery. To *navigate your way to a brighter future* you will need to overcome hurdles, roadblocks and a myriad of other obstacles that can come your way. Unless you are very lucky, it is inevitable there will be some, so be prepared and I will provide you with a winning steer to keep you firmly on track and the right course to achieve a successful outcome.

Whatever stage you are at with your career and for whatever reasons you are attracted to this book, the starting point for any successful career change is to *'let go and look forward'*. This can be a real 'tug of war' so think of your situation as *'work in progress'*.

In this Chapter we will explore:

- Your perspective – what is your outlook right now?
- Understanding and accepting that you must change for change to happen
- Embracing change – knowing when to walk away
- Practical tips when working through career change – how to stay ahead of the game
- The 'emotional roller coaster' – managing the ride and your emotions
- Personal Development – ways to develop a 'toolkit of knowledge' to be the best you can be
- Mindset – how you can change your thinking, to change your career and your 'Toolkit for Life'
- Fear and Focus – how not to let your fear paralyse your career change
- The Law of Attraction – how you can attract positive outcomes

Perspective – What Does Letting Go Mean To You?

To start your journey, you need to consider where you are coming from right now. Is this from a position of:

- Excitement
- Anticipation
- Positivity
- Clarity
- Apprehension
- Anxiety
- Self-doubt
- Chaos
- Fear
- Fog
- Frustration
- Denial
- Stress
- Focus
- Opportunity

The aim of this Chapter is to move you to a desired state of **belief in the Career Navigation Cycle process** to let go and look forward. Consider the PERSPECTIVE acronym and spend a few minutes quietly thinking through what these statements mean to you. As you work your way through the book you will develop and experience these aspects as you navigate each step of the Cycle.

P = *Purposeful focus on your new future*
E = *Enlightenment as you embark on a journey*
R = *Realise and release your potential*
S = Self-reflection to build self-belief
P = *Positive attitude, beliefs and mindset*
E = *Evolving process to achieve your goal*
C = *Create and implement a plan*
T = *Transformational experience*
I = *Imagine limitless possibilities*
V = *Visualise and feel your success*
E = *Evaluate* ***all*** *options and enjoy the process*

Time For Change

"It is not the strongest of the species that survives, nor the most intelligent, but the one most responsive to change."

Charles Darwin, Scientist & Naturalist, 1809-1882

In order to change you must first change

The only thing certain in life is change, as we hear all the time, don't we? A great example is Social Media, which is having a dramatic impact on the world of work, recruitment, networking and job searching. I meet many people who are resisting such an important revolution but ignore this at your peril if you are a serious career professional. Embracing social media is a classic example of where you need to be open and responsive to change. A contact of mine told me of a situation where he was being interviewed for a new job and the HR manager expressed a major concern, as they could not find him on any social networks. The suggestion was that either he was well hidden or a luddite! This was a sharp reality check and needless to say he didn't get the job. Despite such a wakeup call and sharing my insight with them, to my knowledge they have yet to address this need with the obvious consequences. We will explore Social Media in more detail in Chapter 4.

Aside from the coaching I do with professionals and executives, I also regularly run workshops and seminars on how best to use **LinkedIn** for job seekers, career changers and business owners. It is remarkable how many professional people say they don't have a profile on LinkedIn or they have made their profile private, as they don't want their details to be in the public domain. This clearly isn't being responsive to change, is it? Also, how can you possibly be serious about making a career change, finding new employment or starting a new business, if you ignore one of the best tools to help you to be found and achieve your career goals? This isn't exactly professional and certainly not 'letting go' is it?

People often ask me what do you mean by *letting go* and what would I need to let go of? This great quote from Deepak Chopra sums it up perfectly for me:

"In the process of letting go you will lose many things from the past, but you will find yourself."

I spend much time coaching clients to 'let go' and 'look forward', in order to see things from a different perspective. Why? Because this will open up new opportunities in your career and life. This is especially true when facing key change in your life, such as changing career. We all tend to hang onto things which serve no benefit to us in moving forward, although we may not see it this way at the time. These can include negative feelings about the job you loved that changed as a result of new owners or new technology; never achieving the promotion you aspired to and felt you deserved and the classic *'I'm just a generalist'*.

When you are looking at changing careers there are many examples of things you will have to let go of which can hold you back from making a successful change. These are mostly because of your mindset and perceptions, which we will explore in more detail shortly. Here are some examples of 'letting go" that you may also face or struggle with yourself:

Knowing When to Walk Away

Isn't it interesting that at the end of a brilliant 1:1 coaching session, having followed a process (which you will learn more about in Chapter 2) to establish my clients top Values and Needs in their career and life and WHY, one of the revelations from my client was the importance of knowing when to walk away from your situation. The analysis at the end of the Values exercise, helps to isolate very clearly why people have enjoyed certain jobs and not others, which triggered this light bulb moment for them. This data can also be used proactively to 'audit' whether a future job opportunity or any self-employed or freelance project is right for you, so powerful stuff! If you haven't done so already, how clear are you on the right time for you to walk away?

The toxic workplace!

The conversation then moved onto their partner who had recently walked away from their job and other people we both knew who had done the same. They hated their jobs so much it was having a massive negative impact on their lives, making them extremely unhappy, stressed out, and affecting their health and wellbeing. Interestingly a number of these people had talked about the '*toxic work environment*'. Why would you want to continue to work somewhere where each day you are being poisoned? You will come across a number of case studies in the book where you will feel the workplace was definitely toxic!

Do you have the courage to walk away?

I mentioned how proud I was of their partner and also another client who had the courage to walk away from their respective situations. Having walked away they were now both relaxed, positive about the future and had the weight of the world lifted off their shoulders. However, the reality is that many people stick with jobs or careers they hate for way too long because they are frightened of getting out of their comfort zone and facing change. **So, at what point do you decide that enough is enough and you must 'let go' and move on? How bad must it get before you do this?** I have seen many people's relationships break up or become strained as a result of one partner's unhappiness, people's health severely affected and even worse, the inevitable heart attack waiting to happen. You don't want this to be you, do you?

Walk away with some money!

Depending on your level of seniority, you may have the opportunity to walk away from your job with a healthy slug of money, which can be your cushion or 'war chest', if redundancy isn't an option. A mutually beneficial compromise agreement is often the best way to go, if it works for the employee and the employer and both parties can then part on reasonably amicable terms. It is always best to seek independent legal advice in such situations.

Doing what is right for you

One of my clients appears to have worked their exit strategy brilliantly well and achieved exactly what they were looking for in terms of a compromise agreement, which has bought them breathing space to rethink their career and life. Equally I have other clients and know of many other people who have just walked away with nothing, because each day was becoming an ever more painful existence. Waiting to find another job, or the right job, was no longer an option. Ultimately, you must do what is right for you and your situation. However, this involves being honest with yourself and your partner, if you have one. Realistically you are the best person to know when it is right to walk away from your job but it often takes other people you know and trust to help you come to the right conclusion. Money is helpful but it isn't everything. Your health and happiness surely come first, don't they?

Can you begin to imagine now, having the courage and therefore the motivation to 'let go' and walk away from your painful existence to redesign your career and life? How good would that feel?

How important is your age when changing careers?

Interestingly, the Sunday Times did some research on changing careers, in the UK in 2014. I was very proud that my company was chosen as their career change specialist and we had a couple of client case studies featured. What did surprise me were their findings because the research highlighted that the average age people made their first career change was 33-34. The article made me realise that there are a number of trigger points in life when people change careers and the first is often when you are in your early thirties. This is often the point when many people start to challenge what they are doing, why they are doing it and maybe that there is something more fulfilling they can be doing. It is also usually triggered by a shift in your values, i.e. what is important to you in your career and life and why, as we will explore in more depth in Chapter 2. My experience is that people are now making significant career changes at an ever younger age, e.g. the '7 year itch', kicking in after your first job post-graduation. Therefore it is now highly likely the average age for a first career change is around age 29-30. In today's fast paced ever changing digital age, predictions are that people will be changing not just jobs more often but changing careers multiple times also. This links to what I will illustrate throughout the book, i.e. age is no barrier, as you can never be too old or too young to make a winning career change.

By now you should have already completed the 'Current Situation Quiz' in the introduction and will be reasonably clear as to why you now want to change career.

If you haven't completed the quiz yet then it is advisable go back and do this now, as it is really important to understand how you feel about your current work situation and why.

This will then help you to let go, take positive action and know when to walk away.

What you might need to let go

Some examples:

Here are some typical examples I come across all the time, usually related to years of conditioning, old beliefs and negative thinking:

- You don't believe you will ever find fulfilling work
- You are too young/old to change
- You don't believe you can earn enough doing something different?
- You believe you must have another employed job as security is important to you
- You feel guilty about turning your back on all the years of training/learning and qualifications you have achieved to get you to where you are now
- You can't see past your job title e.g. I'm a xyz
- You can't see past your business sector e.g. I have worked in Finance for my entire career so how can I do anything different?
- You will miss your work colleagues if you walk away
- You are frightened to leave your comfort zone

Letting Go – Your Toolkit For Life! The Simplified Law Of Cause And Effect

The common thread that links every element of my Career Navigation Cycle is the need to change your thinking. I have highlighted that to change, you must first change, let go and look forward. *"But how do you do this?" I hear you ask.*

To 'let go and look forward', you must change your perspective and have real focus to be able to unlock and fulfil your potential, open up and see new opportunities, then take the positive action required to make a successful career change. Simple isn't it? If only it was! The good news is that you can make it simple by doing one thing to start the process, which will then create an incredible chain reaction and change your life! Start thinking differently.

In order to transform your thinking, you need a simple but powerful 'template' or mantra to live your life by. This is wonderfully encapsulated by *The Simplified Law of Cause and Effect,* which I have now renamed your *'Toolkit for Life'*, as a result of many clients telling me this is exactly what it is and how it has helped them let go and now fly. So here is your first key tool. Please do not underestimate the power of this mantra 'Toolkit for Life'.

Why is it so powerful? Because... As you journey through your voyage of self-discovery, you will undoubtedly start to experience some of the changes highlighted below. Once you have achieved your desired career and life goals, by working through this book, **you will change your results and ultimately your life!**

In essence, for every cause there is an effect and by changing the cause, you change the effect, i.e. outcome. This simple 'law' is universal and works time and again. Just like the 6 Step SMP Career Navigation Cycle process, there is a natural sequence to work through and once you have learnt it and experienced success, you can do the same again in any situation of change, not just in your career.

Use this 'law' to focus, challenge and motivate yourself to achieve success in your life. We will revisit this 'law' in the Conclusion.

'Toolkit for Life'

When we change our	**THINKING** we change our	**BELIEFS**
When we change our	**BELIEFS** we change our	**EXPECTATIONS**
When we change our	**EXPECTATIONS** we change our	**ATTITUDES**
When we change our	**ATTITUDES** we change our	**FEELINGS**
When we change our	**FEELINGS** we change our	**BEHAVIOUR**
When we change our	**BEHAVIOUR** we change our	**RESULTS**
When we change our	**RESULTS** we change our	**LIFE**

Managing Your Emotions

Everyone is affected differently by changing careers. For many it is highly challenging and stressful and for others it is exciting and stimulating, as I really hope it will be for you. How you manage your emotions will play a big part in how quickly you can *let go and look forward*. **Your mindset will be key to your success**, so say to yourself: *'It's a voyage of self-discovery and I am going to enjoy the journey'*, rather than just focusing on your destination. The Cycle process will help you achieve this but only if you have the right mindset and believe you will ultimately succeed, then take positive action to make it happen.

The Emotional Roller Coaster

There are many change curves and models illustrating what can happen to you as a result of key change in your life. However, I want you to imagine you are on a roller coaster ride with **upward, downward and sideways swings**, as it is rarely the case you will have straight downward then upward swings. Your journey is likely to be an *'emotional roller coaster'* but how you manage your emotions throughout the ride is what counts.

Even if you are excited and energised, it is helpful to understand how the process of change may affect you and what you can do to turn any potentially negative situation into a positive outcome for you.

Depending on your situation, whether you are working at your change whilst still employed, returning to work after a career break or just had enough and jumped ship, your feelings are likely to change dramatically, as you work through the Cycle and experience both positive 'small wins' or negative knock backs. Both are inevitable but managing your negative emotions will have the most impact, especially any loss of confidence and self-esteem, *"The best way to 'let go' is to carefully consider your learning from similar past experiences and apply this to the current situation to propel you forward"*.

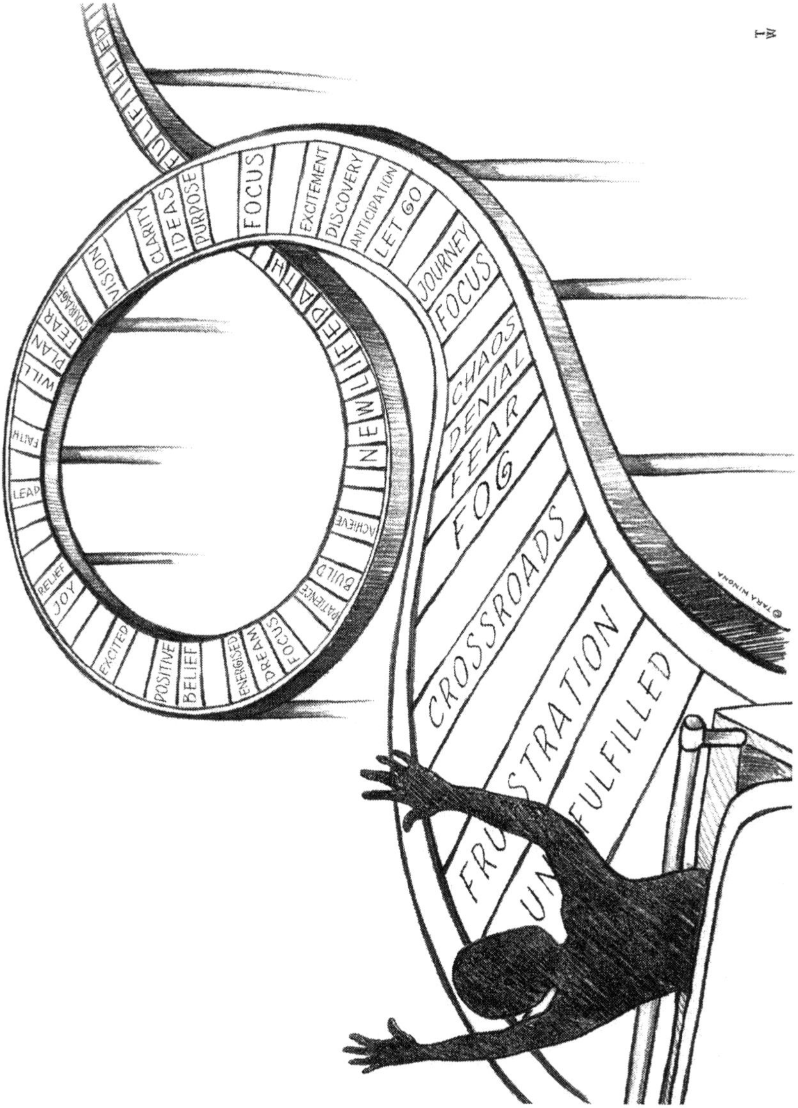
UNFULFILLED
FRUSTRATION
CROSSROADS
FOG
FEAR
DENIAL
CHAOS
FOCUS
JOURNEY
LET GO
ANTICIPATION
DISCOVERY
EXCITEMENT
FOCUS
PURPOSE
IDEAS
CLARITY
VISION
COURAGE
FEAR
PLAN
WILL
FAITH
LEAP
RELIEF
JOY
EXCITED
POSITIVE
BELIEF
ENERGISED
DREAM
FOCUS
PATIENCE
BUILD
ACHIEVE
NEW LIFE PATH
FULFILLED

There Is No Right Or Wrong Way To Feel

There are many individual factors which can affect your thinking, such as how you feel about the questions we looked at in the Introduction, also your personal and financial situation. Therefore 'one size does not fit all'.

For some people, there might be an initial feeling of euphoria at the prospect of following your dream, only to find later that you come crashing down to reality. This is especially so, if making your career change becomes much more difficult than you expected, due to circumstances outside of your control. You will read a great example of this with Mark's Story, at the end of this Chapter.

The Emotional Roller Coaster illustrates what many people go through when experiencing career change. Where are you on the roller coaster ride right now?

Career Change Strategies – Do's

Regardless of your situation and how you may be feeling, I will share with you some effective strategies to help you move safely round the ***Emotional Roller Coaster*** to ultimately achieve a successful career change.

Live your dream – do what you want to!

This might be the first time in your life you have the opportunity to take stock and review what **you** really want to do with your career and life. Accept that you are at a career crossroads, embrace change and your voyage of self-discovery to live your dreams so you end up doing work **you want and love**! You also have an opportunity to revisit any *'what if'* thoughts you may have had from the past e.g. *what if* I set up my own business, *what if* I change career to become...?

Manage your career change as a project - make the journey step by step

From now on, treat your career change, as a transition project and you will be far more successful. You are a *work in progress*, ready to explore new opportunities. As things start to evolve, you can set aims, objectives, milestones and outcomes which you can constantly review and revise to keep you on track to achieve your end goal. As with many things in life, what gets measured gets done!

Talk to people - it's good to talk!

Don't forget there are always other people who have trodden the path before you to achieve a successful career change. It pays to talk to people who have and got through the other side and are now thriving. What did they do and learn? I will be sharing my experiences with you and case studies of other people, but it is likely you also know people. Find them and talk things through. You never know what may come from this.

Believe most people genuinely want to help

Taking my last point, so often I have heard people say 'I didn't want to bother so and so as I know they are always busy'. Do yourself a favour and change your beliefs around this, as the majority of people are only too pleased to help if they can. This is something I learnt very early on in my transition, which was a very pleasant surprise. Why do most people want to help? Simple... human nature being what it is, people don't like to see you unhappy or disadvantaged and they also might consider how they would like people to react if they were in your position. Therefore, if they can help in any way they mostly will, with the caveat from my list of don'ts, i.e. 'don't dump your baggage on others'!

Get the right support networks - surround yourself with positive people and people who want you to succeed

We will explore the importance of a positive mindset in detail in this Chapter. The key here is positive people radiate positive energy, which becomes infectious. To work through your career change you need positive energy by the bucket load, so you need to be around positive people who will boost you up rather than bring you down. Bear in mind it may not always be your nearest and dearest. Even if they are full of support and well meaning, they are sometimes (not always) way too close and if they are overly fearful for the future, they may hinder rather than help you. **My experience has proven it is often the most unlikely people who can help unlock the key to your future.** Think about who are the valued and trusted contacts you have made throughout your career and your networks in general? Now is the time to start rebuilding and developing your networks both online and offline. We will revisit the importance of networks and networking throughout the book, especially in Step 4 of the Cycle when 'exploring opportunities'

Consider opportunities for changing careers within your existing organisation

I highlighted in the Introduction, how I had changed jobs numerous times with my previous employer. I now realise that I actually changed careers multiple times too, as I moved into completely different roles away from my travel background into Operations, Project Management and Reward & Benefits, none of which I had any previous experience. Likewise you might be able to do the same if you are frustrated in your job but still enjoy working for your organisation. In Chapter 4 we will look at 'secondments' (a temporary transfer to another position) and 'redeployment' (placing people from redundant roles into another vacancy often as an alternative to termination of employment) as true opportunities for the future.

Get independent financial advice

It makes good sense to review and plan your finances as part of any career change strategy. This way you can plan ahead for a better financial cushion or to maximize your existing savings and investments, to give you more breathing space. To be able to work through your career change with the minimum of financial restrictions will provide you with increased confidence that you can achieve a successful change. You should always seek advice from a trusted or recommended source to determine the best options to manage your personal finances. You may also want to do the same for your pension, if you have one. We will revisit the importance of this when re-evaluating your finances in Chapter 2.

Celebrate 'small wins'

Achieving a successful career change is like any project with a lifespan. I always stress the importance and have proven with many clients the benefits of looking for 'small wins', so you can see you are making progress towards your goal. This might be making new connections, really letting go, feeling more confident, getting invited to interviews for completely different jobs, getting your LinkedIn profile into good shape, taking the first steps to setting up your own business, winning your first client etc. For each 'small win' why not give yourself a small 'reward', e.g. a meal out, some 'retail therapy', a bottle of wine or something to make you feel good and positive about yourself. Be proud, as you are making progress and that should feel good, don't you think?

Develop resilience – after any knockback so you still see your career change as an opportunity

At this stage you might be thinking it is easy for me to say this but how do I get myself to a better place if I keep coming up against obstacles? The easiest and best solution is to stop, take stock of the situation, consider the positive learning from this and other similar past situations and apply this knowledge to overcoming any barriers to achieve that end goal. However, don't worry, as most of this Chapter will cover exercises, strategies, practical tips and case studies to help you think differently. You can start to let go and look forward and ultimately tackle your career change in a new light. Also, there is always light at the end of the tunnel, isn't there?

Personal Development

"If you wish to achieve worthwhile things in your personal and career life, you must become a worthwhile person in your own self development"

Brian Tracy, Professional Speaker, Best Selling Author, Entrepreneur and Success Expert

Many people feel that by getting more professional qualifications it will help them in their career. This depends entirely on what you are planning to do next and the relevance of the qualifications gained. I have met many people who have invested large sums of money on their professional development only to find it took them up a blind alley. However, working on your personal development will help you for the rest of your life, regardless of what you do. We will be looking at ways to develop and grow personally, useful materials to motivate and inspire you and looking at relevant professional help for your needs.

Work On Your Personal Development & Growth

Think of Personal Development like going to the gym but instead of developing your muscles you are developing your mind. Finding the tools and materials that work best for you will help you learn how to develop a successful mindset, improve your confidence and self-esteem and become the best person you can be. Imagine how this will impact positively on your outlook on life and likewise your career? How good would this be? I have provided some useful tips to help you on your way:

Reading inspiring material (like this book), listening and watching personal development CDs/DVDs, streaming audio and video files (e.g. Podcasts, Youtube clips), attending motivational workshops, seminars and courses can all help to inspire you, teach you new skills, learn success strategies and change your thinking to help you make your career change. I don't believe in harbouring regrets but wonder how my life would have shaped up if I had learnt some of these key strategies when I was younger. At least I can now share them with family, friends, my clients and of course you!

One of my all-time favourite audio books is ***The New Psychology of Achievement*** by world renowned psychologist, author, speaker and success guru, Brian Tracy. I personally love Brian Tracy for his amazing ability to translate highly complex aspects of psychology into simple practical solutions to achieve success in your life. Brian Tracy's audio programmes and work have acted as a mentor to me, providing me with great insight, which has inspired and influenced me personally and also many of my clients, with whom I have shared his work. I am therefore truly proud and humbled that Brian has personally endorsed this book.

Another book I recommend highly is *'Who Moved My Cheese'* by Dr Spencer Johnson: an amazingly clever book which uses cheese as a metaphor for what you want to have in life. It is just under 100 pages so you can read it cover to cover in no time. The book has achieved 'cult' status with organisations and individuals around the globe, as people are drawn to stories with metaphors as a way of learning to manage change and build self-esteem.

I have also learnt that a key factor in achieving personal success is to take some risks which push you out of your comfort zone. People who have high self-esteem take risks and people who take risks have high self-esteem. We will be revisiting this throughout the book.

To summarise the power of personal development, in the words of the late, great Jim Rohn (psychologist and mentor to Tony Robbins) *"One of the keys to a successful life is to work harder on yourself than you do on your job. Working on your job will earn your living whereas working on yourself can earn you a fortune!"*

Get Professional Help – Hire A Career Coach It Will Pay You!

This book will help you coach yourself and will be a brilliant guide to *winning through career change and navigating your way to a brighter future.* However, a good career coach can support all the good work you will do in this book. They will act as a catalyst for your change to challenge you and your thinking, get you focused, unlock your potential and hidden talents so you can gain clarity, build a vision for your future, boost your confidence, keep you motivated and on track to achieve your goals.

Friends and family and other valued contacts are important to help you through your career change. However, a good Career Coach, besides being an expert, is also independent and impartial. Therefore they can support you without the same emotional connection. The benefits they can provide to you will have a knock on effect to your family and support networks in general; as they see you become more positive, focused and moving forward with a real sense of purpose. Consider working with a Career Coach as a positive investment in your future. You are far more likely to make a speedier career change or transition, so will earn back the money you paid out much quicker to get a return on your investment. Alternatively, if you enjoy learning online in your own time and at your own pace, you may wish to consider investing in online career change programmes such as my innovative *'Navigate Your Way To A Brighter Future – 6 steps to transform your career and life'*. This programme has been described as *'not just inspirational but transformational'* and is deliberately planned to work brilliantly in tandem with this book by bringing it to life.

Getting Into The Right Mindset

Looking back on your life and career, I can pretty much guarantee that when things went well you had a positive mindset and you were determined to succeed. Winning through career change is no different - it is all about having the right mindset!

Success guru, Brian Tracy says in his *New Psychology of Achievement* audio book, *"You always perform on the outside based on the way you think about yourself on the inside. You become what you think about most of the time. Change your thinking and you change your life".*

We will be exploring much about the importance of mindset and changing your thinking throughout this book, as it is key to your successful career transition and success in life. **You can no doubt now see why the 'Toolkit for Life', earlier in the Chapter, is such a powerful mantra.**

PIT STOP WINNING STEER

If you are looking to make a total career change, you are unlikely to have much of the information or tools you need at this early step of the Cycle.

The Career Navigation Cycle process is designed to challenge your thinking and to give you a real sense of purpose. Only by following the natural flow of steps will this help you to evolve, develop and refine your plan as you progress round the Cycle and develop that winning mindset and achieve results.

Be patient and follow the process!

Reframe Your Thinking To Respond Differently

My years as a Career Coach have taught me that the nature of my previous work and the skills I acquired are relevant and in demand in pretty much any sector. People often become blinkered, so don't see the bigger picture of their transferable skills and true marketability (we will explore this in Chapter 3). Your inherent talents and developed skills mean that there are always new opportunities and possibilities to be explored. Remember just because you have always done something or similar jobs before doesn't mean you can't do anything else. You always have a CHOICE!

I remember speaking at a major careers event for the medical profession. My theme was around challenging yourself to be open to new opportunities outside of the medical profession in light of the changing Health Service agenda. I had a queue of people waiting to see me after the seminar. One was a GP who was looking most concerned. He told me he had only ever been a GP so how could he possibly do anything else? Conscious of the long queue, waiting patiently, I asked a key question to help him on the way; *'Do you want to continue working with people?'* The look of shock and horror on his face was unbelievable *'God no, I hate people!'* He was clearly in the wrong job and may not have realised it before, but he started his career transition journey there and then.

The good news is that it is never too late to change career, regardless of what you are doing now or have done previously.

What you can and must do is to reframe and take your positive learning and experiences from the past and bring these with you to help you move forward. When you combine these with a positive mindset, you have a winning combination. I'm sure this sounds more encouraging, doesn't it?

Controlling Your Own Self Talk & Inner Dialogue

Reframing your thinking will also make you aware of what you say and how you say it. I learnt very early on in my transition about the importance of positive language and the power of communication. Learning to manage and control your inner dialogue (what you are thinking and saying to yourself) is a key part of the reframing process.

Having now gained an understanding of the importance of your mindset and reframing, do you see your current career situation and life as a threat or an opportunity? Ask yourself this key question:

Are you behaving like a 'victim'; constantly bemoaning your fate to everyone you meet, so life passes you by like being an extra in your own movie?

Or

Do you see yourself as being the architect of your own new future, playing the starring role in your own movie, taking control of your career and making it happen? I'm sure you will agree this sounds much more appealing, doesn't it?

The importance of what you say, how you say it and to whom

The way you communicate plays a significant part in ultimately achieving a successful career change or transition. You never know who will unlock the key to your future, as I have mentioned and will continue to do so throughout the book.

Communication becomes all important when networking (we will cover this in step 4), at interviews or for any informal interactions with people you meet in any situation. Remember, you never get a second chance to make a first impression, so make sure it is the right one for you!

Let's say you meet someone socially and they ask, *'what do you do'*? Do you say *'I am working for x as a y but hate it'* then proceed to tell them about your woes? If so, this is not uncommon in my experience. Instead, try hard to change your thinking and replace such comments with ***'I am currently working for x as a y but looking to change career and do work I love'*** or, if applicable ***'I am in transition and exploring new opportunities'***.

Let's say you were in HR. You could reframe your statement to *'I am an HR Manager. However, in all honesty I feel it is time to change and I am now looking for a new challenge'*. I'm sure you would rather help this person, wouldn't you?

Adopting a positive mindset and reframing your thinking means that you are far more likely to use positive language and gain a helpful response. Listen to the way you speak to others and notice their reaction. This will speak volumes about how you may need to change your language and tone to gain your desired reaction or response. Ask friends and family for honest feedback in helping you to identify any negative words or phrases that you may be using. Then make a list and try reframing them into positive ones. The following case study is an excellent example of how you can achieve this.

Dee's Story

Dee is a very talented lady who is highly memorable for many reasons. As soon as she arrived at my workshop her personality lit up the room. She was clearly excited at the prospect of the workshop, came across as very bubbly, personable, intelligent and had some wonderfully creative ideas. Unfortunately, her ideas were being quashed by many of the people around her. This was seriously damaging her confidence, self-esteem and causing her to question her ability and beliefs. Dee left the workshop really motivated and determined to get her career back on track. I felt with the right support and guidance she would be a star.

A year later she resurfaced after a job abroad didn't work out and things had gone from bad to worse. Her marriage had been a disaster and she had given up her career to play the dutiful housewife. She was now in her early thirties, single, living at home again and it was two years since she had had a 'proper job'. Dee could not see the wood for the trees; her confidence and self-worth were shot to pieces. She was determined to get her career and life back on track and borrowed the money from her parents to invest in her future with a coaching programme, which you can only admire her for. This made me even more determined to help her succeed!

Dee made excellent progress from the career coaching. She was energised, wanted to make up for lost time and the creative ideas were starting to flow again. She really associated with my Career Navigation Cycle process and was keen to unlock her potential, her passions and establish her true marketability to find work she loved.

However, what struck me was how she would make a positive statement then almost immediately doubt herself using negative language and "but" time and again. What was her problem? Dee admitted she was struggling with her 'self-talk'. Although outwardly trying to be positive, the voice in her head was challenging her which resulted in negative statements flowing forth. This was not surprising considering what she had been through. If you also find yourself experiencing similar issues, you will be pleased to know there is a solution.

I got Dee to focus on controlling self-talk by disciplining herself to reframe the negative inner voice as soon as she felt it coming. Also, to listen very closely to what she was saying, how this was coming across and how people reacted to what she said. Experts suggest it takes 30 days to break a habit through sustained reframing and effort and she was up for the challenge! Eventually Dee managed to discipline and self-coach herself so she could stop the negative self-talk as soon as she felt it coming on. You would see her smile which acknowledged she had managed to take control of her inner dialogue. The impact was amazing and her language changed completely with excitement replacing self-doubts. It was a joy talking with her on the phone. She would tell me about all the exciting things that were happening to her and seemed bemused at why this was suddenly the case.

What Dee failed to recognise was that her new positive focus and vibrant energy was manifesting more of what she wanted in her life instead of what she didn't want, as you will read about shortly in the Law of Attraction. Good things started to happen for her and she quickly started turning her life around. A massive mindset shift was focusing on doing work she loved, rather than what was expected of her by friends and family, thus becoming the architect of her own future. Dee has since had the confidence to make a number of career changes, mainly different aspects of developing a portfolio career - trading commodities, Forex trading, property development, consultancy and recruitment projects. She has also since moved on with her life and remarried.

Career Change Strategies- Don'ts

The following list is to help you avoid slipping into a negative mindset, which will only lead you to doubt yourself as did Dee.

Don't live in the past – *"You cannot recreate the past but you can create a great new future"*

Living in the past will achieve nothing, other than causing pain and frustration, as you can no longer influence the past. Having made the decision to change career focus on the present and creating your new future and not the past.

If you have already left your job, you might be missing the colleagues you worked with and the daily banter and interaction. This can often be difficult to replace quickly if at all. However, this doesn't mean that you can't still socialise with them, as long as there isn't a conflict of interest.

Don't 'beat yourself up'

Let's not beat about the bush. Changing careers isn't an easy process and you need to be focused, positive and resilient. Unless you are super proactive or exceptionally 'lucky', it will take time, hard graft and bags of commitment and determination to achieve your successful career change. Therefore if you were hoping for a quick escape route from your current or previous 'grind', you may be upset. If you follow the rest of these strategies it will help you 'let go and look forward', as quickly as possible, bearing in mind we are all different.

You may well get self-doubts or 'hit the metaphorical wall'. So many of my clients say to me: *'I don't understand why I am feeling this way, as I am usually a very positive person'.* My typical answer is *'what you are describing is a natural reaction to what you are going through, if you have never experienced changing careers'.*

You may feel unhappy, frustrated, and fearful that you are finding it difficult to work out what you want to do or how to achieve this and any other negative emotions, The important thing is not to 'beat yourself up' over this.

Another important consideration is you may get 'waves of emotion', just like any other change process, so just when you thought you had let go, other emotions come back to haunt you. Many people will experience an emotional roller coaster but accept this and learn to ride it out.

Don't dump your 'baggage' on other people

If you are finding making your career change exceptionally challenging and frustrating, or you absolutely hate your current job and can't wait to jump ship, it might be a difficult time for you but most people don't want to hear all your woes of the world. If you are constantly projecting a negative persona, people won't thank you for this. More than likely, they will turn their back on you instead and you don't want this, do you?

Don't become an island

Depending on your situation you may not want too many people to know that you are looking to change careers, especially if you are setting up in competition to your current employer. However, I have met many people who isolate themselves during their transition. To be successful now is the time to 'be out there' talking to people and making things happen, not hiding in your shell and then trying to surprise people.

Don't neglect your health

Without your health you have nothing. I've come across many people who have been working at their career change while still having their day job and have been blighted by poor health, as they have neglected their need for rest and recreation. All work and no exercise or play is a recipe for disaster! Likewise, if you made a conscious decision to give up your job and focus on your career change, then you also need to find time to exercise, relax and eat healthily. If you are the sort of person who thrives on a sporty or healthy lifestyle, to stop now will impact in a negative way just at the time you need a boost. Even if you aren't into sport, physical exercise creates endorphins that improve your wellbeing and physical stamina, so at this key time, just going for walks and clearing your mind are great ways to help stimulate your creativity or let go. This point is exemplified by my client, Steve, who during his career transition initially neglected himself. Through a combination of exercise and a healthy eating regime, he lost over 2 stones and felt much better about himself and ready to go out and meet people, network and gain the support he needed to ultimately achieve his successful career change.

Don't turn down people's help

If people you value and trust, and other people who have a genuine desire to help you, are offering to help, take it, even if it means 'eating humble pie'. You may never get the offer again and you don't want to regret this, do you?

Don't join the negative brigade

It is all too easy to wallow in your own self-pity and seek refuge with others struggling to make their own career changes. This will only bring you down and prolong your ability to let go and make a successful change. This is not the 'support group' you want or need right now or ever for that matter, is it?

Don't spend your life on the internet

If you are planning a career change, you have much work to do before you can even start to think about your next career. You will soon come to realise, by reading this book, that there is little or no benefit to spending hours of your time job searching on the internet. This is all too easy but it is time that you can use far more productively working your way through the 6 steps of the Cycle process and the exercises in this book.

Don't try to short cut the process or work on your CV yet

The biggest mistake you can make at this stage is to try to circumnavigate the process, thinking that you will be smart and save time. I have seen this happen but unfortunately is unlikely to work as **the reality is more haste = less speed!** A good example is a client who hadn't realised or accepted they were at a career crossroads but it was evident to me from how they described their situation. I suggested they take out my Breakthrough Career Development Coaching programme and work through the 6 Step Cycle process, to take stock and then decide how to take their career forward. They instead insisted on having impromptu coaching sessions every time they wanted to address their unhappiness and feelings at work or saw a new job opportunity advertised. As a result they ended up paying considerably more than if they had heeded my advice whilst also elongating the time to get to where they wanted to be, at a point of clarity. Having reached frustration point, they finally accepted they needed to work through the Cycle process and start at Step 1, working through methodically, rather than trying to shortcut by being scattergun. They have since reaped the benefits, as the journey has challenged their thinking in many ways, resulting in a whole new perspective on their career and life in general.

So, you don't want to waste time firing out your CV to the world until you have decided what you want to do and have done the work to ensure that your CV is targeted and focused and you have a clear sense of purpose, do you? You will then hit the target and avoid all the frustration that this 'scattergun' approach fails to achieve.

Remember you cannot hit a target you cannot see, so what benefit is job searching on the internet or firing out your CV to recruiters or employers if you haven't worked through what you want to do next and why? Following the Cycle process means less haste but ultimately more speed, as your focus will be where it matters. Alternatively, you may be working through the process and thinking you want to start your own business, in which case you are unlikely to need a CV in the traditional sense at all. You may need to focus on other aspects such as your online profile on LinkedIn, which we will revisit in Chapter 4.

Don't procrastinate

Having decided to change career. Learn to be proactive and to take control of your career. The worst scenario is to suddenly spring into life only when you become desperate, as your current job has become totally unbearable or you have spent your 'war chest', if taken time out and feel obligated to start being proactive. This is a recipe for disaster. By following the Cycle process and doing the exercises in this book you will keep focused and on track.

Don't think you already know it all

Even if this is not your first experience of changing careers, your thoughts and feelings might be very different this time round. Also, **the world of work has moved on and there are so many new possibilities and opportunities which may not have been available to you previously.** Most importantly, you won't have had the benefit of my Career Navigation Cycle process to guide you before. This may help you arrive at completely different conclusions about what you might want to do next, so you could easily end up taking a very different direction to what you expected.

Don't take the first job offer that comes along

This is a common mistake, mainly because you feel flattered, relieved or you are pandering to your ego because it proves you can make a successful change. Unless you have an immediate financial need and cannot wait to complete the Cycle, or it looks an absolute perfect fit, with your Values and Needs (Chapter 2) I would urge caution, as you could be jumping from the 'frying pan into the fire'. Follow the 6 Step process and you will find the job, career or work **you really want!**

Perception Versus Reality

In terms of mindset, one of the biggest roadblocks that people face when looking at career transition is all the limiting beliefs they put in their own way. Henry Ford, the American industrialist and founder of the Ford Motor Company, challenged perception when he said, *'Whether you think you can or you can't you are right'*. In other words, it is you who holds the key. It is now time to challenge your mindset, as you will often see things that are your perception rather than the reality. I'm sure you agree that it is so much easier to see things and behaviours in other people than we can see in ourselves. How often do you give advice to family, friends or work colleagues about their situations but you can't see the wood for the trees yourself?

Imagine one of your friends is telling you about their career change situation. They then hit you with some of these statements:

- I'm not sure I have the experience or the confidence to do that type of job
- I like the sound of the job but wouldn't know how to use the technology or systems they have
- There will be more experienced people than me going for the job so there's no point in me applying
- They will think I am over or under qualified
- I am interested in doing something different, but I haven't had an interview in years
- I don't know how or where to start looking for jobs
- My age will go against me
- I like the idea of starting my own business but don't have the skills or know how to start

Consider how you would address these statements **Will you:**

Tell your friend that you feel they are wasting their time and to forget the idea of changing career as they are better off doing a similar job to the one they are currently doing

Or

Challenge why they are making these statements and give them encouragement that they have far more to offer than they think.

And

Ask them for more information about the job or career they are considering and try to allay their fears?

I'm sure you chose the latter two statements, didn't you? This is exactly the thought process I will be taking you through in this book to help you to reframe your thinking. I have always been a firm believer that having a positive attitude and mindset, combined with great personal attributes such as: passion, hunger, desire, enthusiasm, energy and drive, can win the day against more experienced and qualified competition. This is a key learning point; **don't let your negative perceptions stop you from following your passions or dream.**

The following case study is without doubt of one of the most extreme examples of reframing I have ever come across. Alison was at a huge disadvantage, as she was traumatised by an unexpected redundancy, so initially held back by many negative emotions, especially fears. Having reframed her situation, she then made a dramatic and swift career change. Her transformation was truly remarkable; from a jabbering wreck at the start of her first session to winning through career change in only around 7 weeks!

How long does it take to make a successful career change?

There is no right or wrong answer to this key question, which you may well be asking, except to say it isn't as vague as the 'how long is a piece of string' analogy. I always ask potential new clients what their timescale to achieve their change is. I have had answers ranging from a ridiculous four weeks to more typically six months to a year. Everybody's situation is different and the most important point is to be realistic. In my experience this means a minimum of 3 months and depending on your situation, anything between 6 months to a year. Your timescale will depend on a number of factors, e.g.

- How much time you have to devote to your career change
- How much 'risk' you are prepared to take
- How focused you are
- How proactive you are
- Whether you are working at your change alone or with a Career Coach
- Last but certainly not least, your mindset/belief to make your change happen

Quickest Ever Career Change!

Alison's Story

Alison was on an outplacement programme with me and thought 'the end of the world had come as we know it' when I first met her. She was rightly concerned at what the future held as she had a young family and her husband was on a low income. How she made such a dramatic career change from an office based senior Admin role to becoming a Teaching Assistant in her local school, is testimony to the Career Navigation Cycle process and what happens when you reframe your thinking and change your mindset.

Her story provides some great learning points and practical tips. Alison was, clearly suffering from shock, traumatised by her situation and spent much of her first session in floods of tears. She was bitter and angry and needed a safe place to let all her angst out. It was important that she 'let go' of this emotional turmoil before we could really start moving forward. The reality:

When I questioned her about her job and how happy she had been, she admitted she had been quietly looking for other jobs for a while, as she felt stale and bored. However, the location suited her as did her part time hours so she could take her kids to school and organise with other parents for them to be collected.

She had also worked with her company for 17 years so didn't really see herself moving anywhere else and she didn't know what other job she could do. As you will come to realise, this is one of the most common 'limiting beliefs' which I will dispel throughout this book. What really upset Alison was having the rug pulled from under her, when she least expected it, rather than leaving of her own choice.

The Reframe

Coaching Alison to 'let go' and start to see things from a new perspective, quickly enabled her to admit her redundancy was actually a blessing in disguise because of the following points:

1. She had a great chance to look for new opportunities which she hadn't actively been doing before. Although Alison was frustrated, like most people, she had been sitting tight in her comfort zone. Now she had no excuse to not break out and explore doing work she loved!

2. Alison had the benefit of a reasonable redundancy pay off, so the family would be ok financially for a while, which is always reassuring.

3. She had an opportunity to re-evaluate her whole family situation, career and work-life balance.

4. Re-evaluating their situation proved that even if she decided to take a lower paid job with less hours, this would benefit her husband who would be able to do more overtime, which could then increase their overall family income. This was a win-win situation.

5. Working through the Cycle, Alison came to realise that she did have some great skills and attributes and was highly marketable.

Therefore, she could now look at a career change with a fresh pair of eyes. She often helped out at her kids' school and maybe this was an opportunity to tap into her passion of working with young children? Having understood what was important to her and why (Step 2), who she was and what she had to offer (Step 3) this gave her the confidence to reframe and see an opportunity rather than a threat. She quickly 'let go' and her progress was amazingly swift. By following steps 1-3 of the Cycle, which you will also do soon, things became clearer and she developed a real sense of purpose. With her new found confidence and self-belief, she started to project a positive persona and things started to happen for her. Much to her surprise Alison landed a great role at her daughter's school, which was a multiple 'win' situation. Her daughter thought it was great that Mum was working in her school, her husband got to do more overtime, the Deputy Head could see her potential to progress to future bigger jobs within the school and it solved the school run challenge!

Key learning

Within the space of a couple of months, Alison had completely turned her life and career around! She is living proof that you should never rule yourself out of certain jobs because your perception is you don't have the 'right' skills or because you may not have the confidence or self-belief to sell yourself. With the right mindset, belief and positive actions, anything is possible within reason! A negative mindset will only make for frustration and this will increase the time it will take to win through your career change. Remember 'You are what you think and feel', which we will return to shortly when looking at the Law of Attraction.

Fear And Focus

"The only thing we have to fear is fear itself - nameless, unreasoning, unjustified terror which paralyses needed efforts to convert retreat into advance."

Franklin D Roosevelt - First Inaugural Address, March 4, 1933

What stops most people ever getting to the starting line in the first place to change careers? Or, having got off the starting blocks to then move forward positively to achieve a successful change? Typically moving out of your comfort zone and **fear is the culprit**. In this section we will discuss fear; fear of the unknown, fear of failure and even fear of success.

Turning Fear Into Focus

Looking back, I now know that fear of success was one of my biggest fears when I set up my business. It may sound silly but I was fearful that my business might become too big, take over my life and I wouldn't be able to do the things I had left the world of employment for and would lose the freedom that I was longing for. I have come to learn that this was a classic limiting belief as there are always ways to combat such situations and anyway what a great problem to have!

When my business did take off and we got involved with some big projects, I had to reframe as I couldn't do everything myself. I had to let go and really enjoyed the process of recruiting some brilliant associates who ran workshops and 1:1 coaching sessions for me, while I was seeing my own personal clients and developing the business. This was the best thing that could have happened for me and my business and became a win-win situation. I was providing some great people with work they loved and many have become personal friends. I now look closely at the client's needs before deciding whether it should be me or one of my team who does the work, so my company business is no longer dependent on me.

The table below shows two acronyms for FEAR. The left side of the table illustrates how most people's perception of fear is unreal, but the perception stops you from taking action. The right side of the table is fear with reframed thinking, making it something you can tackle head on.

FEAR	***INTO***	**FOCUS**
F alse	**V**	**F** eeling
E vidence	**V**	**E** xcited
A ppearing	**V**	**A** nd
R eal	**V**	**R** eady

Jane's Story

When I first met Jane she was in a bad place. By her own admission she was a highly confident person, who had always achieved whatever she set out to. She had developed her career to a high executive level in a global plc, was previously full of energy and ideas and always had a sense of purpose. As a result of key changes within the company she was given a new challenge and soon afterwards a new boss. This was not a role she felt comfortable or happy doing as she was not playing to her undoubted strengths. Her new boss had a completely different mindset and values to what she was accustomed to. Jane was also spending an inordinate amount of time travelling and being away from her family, something that she was finding increasingly uncomfortable at a time when her children were coming up to major exams.

For the first time in her career she started to feel very differently about her company and was rapidly losing her confidence, energy and self-esteem. As difficult as it was for her, she knew that if she could not get back into a role that she wanted, she had to leave and move on as her situation was becoming untenable.

She could not see herself moving to a competitor and yet when I questioned her it became clear that she liked the idea of being her own boss and even had a 'patchy' vision for starting her own company. However, her biggest concern and the main reason for contacting me was in her words – "I don't know how I will survive without the corporate umbrella around me".

What I discovered through the coaching was that FEAR was at the heart of what was really holding her back. This was all the usual fears e.g. fear of the unknown, fear of failure (something she had never experienced), fear of not being able to reposition or reinvent herself, damage to her personal brand, fear of not being able to earn enough and so on.

Jane was astounded when I told her I had gone through all these self-doubts and fears and so do most of my clients. Relating her situation back to the previous exercise, were these perceptions or reality? Jane had proved throughout her career that once she had a goal, real focus, clarity and belief, she was capable of achieving anything, so her thinking was clearly an emotional response and perception rather than reality.

With this is mind, I coached Jane on to how to reframe her fear and turn this into focus, using the two FEAR acronyms. The result was quite remarkable and had an immediate and dramatic impact. As a constant reminder to help her, she made a business card with her new business idea on the front and the two FEAR acronyms on the reverse. We did much work around her values, true marketability and personal brand, all of which you will cover in the next two Chapters. As a result, she regained her confidence, self-belief and her sense of purpose. In her words 'The clouds lifted and my dark world turned into a glorious bright future. Don't delay, turn your fear into focus and take charge of your own future doing something you love'.

Jane set up her own consultancy, which has since evolved into a number of different business ventures. She has become a sought after business and IT change consultant, programme manager, coach and mentor. Most importantly Jane has long banished her fears to become the architect of her own future, now living life on her terms and never been happier!

✎ *Exercise – Fearful Statements*

I will now share with you this simple but effective way to reframe your fears using two different acronyms for FEAR from the fear into focus table. Here are some examples of 'fearful' statements I often hear from clients together with ways to turn them around.

Now you have heard Jane's story, consider carefully what fears may be holding you back and WHY and have a go at turning them into something positive. Understanding WHY you are so fearful is so important, as this is often where you will uncover that, like Jane, your fear is mostly perception rather than reality. Of course we are all fearful of certain things and you might be so of a career change, thinking this might not work for you. However, what if it does? How great would that be? I love the sentiments of enigmatic author and blogger, Seth Godin who encourages people to *"dance with fear and opportunity"*. Maybe this approach will change your views on fear? I hope so.

Fear	Evidence	Focus
I'm too old	Many employers now want younger candidates who have a more up to date skill set and cost less	I have a wide range of business and life skills, a positive attitude and years of experience and can bring real value to a company or a business of my own
I won't come across well at interviews	I have never had a formal interview or haven't had one in years	I need help and support to hone my interview skills, so I can sell myself really effectively – I do have lots to offer
I feel like I have become my job title	I have always done this type of work so don't know anything else	I need to understand what is important to me in a future job or career, identify my talents and transferable skills and establish my true marketability

The Law Of Attraction

To put this Chapter into context, one of the fundamental principles of quantum physics, as told by scientists, is that all life is vibrating energy. Therefore, what energy you put out to the universe is manifested back as a result of your thoughts and feelings. Simply put, if you have a negative mindset, are feeling bad about yourself, have self-doubts about your abilities, job or career prospects and you focus on what you don't want in life, then this is what will manifest itself back to you and you won't get the promotion or job you want and your negativity will come back to haunt you. Think like the victim, behave like one and you will become the victim.

Conversely, positive energy will attract the same, which is just what you need to win through career change. Positive people radiate energy to those around them, often lighting up their own and others' lives, resulting in positive outcomes. If you have a positive mindset and you are always focusing on what you do want in life, believe in yourself and your ability to make things happen, this is what will manifest for you in the areas of life that you focus on. I'm sure you would rather help the positive person who fuels you with positive energy, than the negative person who drains you, wouldn't you? We will be revisiting this Law and other important laws of success and achievement later in the book.

Michael's Wakeup Call!

A wonderful example which encompasses much of what we have covered in this Chapter; letting go and looking forward, the Law of Attraction, reframing, turning fear into focus, changing mindset and the power of language was Michael. Following major restructuring in his organisation, I was coaching him to achieve a successful

A wonderful example which encompasses much of what we have covered in this Chapter; letting go and looking forward, the Law of Attraction, reframing, turning fear into focus, changing mindset and the power of language was Michael. Following major restructuring in his organisation, I was coaching him to achieve a successful career transition and change. Having explained the Career Navigation Cycle process, the importance of letting go and looking forward and how positive mindset and what you say, how you say it and to whom can influence your outcomes, I had noticed that Michael's language was constantly negative and that he seemed determined to dump his baggage on anyone who would listen, e.g. how badly the company was treating him, how it was getting him down etc. etc. He seemed oblivious to the fact that many of his colleagues had also picked up on his negative persona and were clearly not impressed!

I coached him to become aware of his language, the impact his negativity was having on people around him and how this was very definitely not helpful to his cause. We agreed that moving forward we would now only focus on positives, especially as his company was investing considerable time and money providing career transition support for him, something not all companies feel obliged to offer.

When I met Michael a couple of weeks later for a follow up in a 1:1 session, I shall never forget his opening welcome... 'Steve you will never believe what happened to me following our last session'. Michael went on to share that he really hadn't realised the extent of his negative feelings and persona as a result of the restructuring. The reaction of his colleagues and my coaching was the 'wakeup call' he needed. To his credit, he decided he must change and he had taken on board how he first needed to change his mindset and work at becoming positive when meeting people, even family and friends and in informal situations.

It transpired that he bumped into an old contact and they went for a beer. They were catching up and Michael explained his situation and "how he was going through career transition and exploring new opportunities".

The specialist field of engineering he had been working in for many years was no longer ideal for him; he was not getting any younger and didn't want to take on anything so physical again.

He was therefore looking to change career and explore new opportunities. He told his friend that he'd done some teaching earlier in his career and was wondering if he could share his wealth of knowledge and experience in a teaching capacity at a college, to benefit engineers of the future. His friend was so impressed by this positive thinking that he immediately said he would be happy to introduce Michael to a good contact of his at a local college. The rest is history and he was at the point of being offered a teaching position when I met him for his final coaching session.

This was another remarkable mindset shift, which was also one of the quickest career change success stories I can remember, especially for someone the 'wrong side of fifty'. Most importantly, Michael made a specific point of telling me his success would never have happened if he had maintained his negative mindset and how this positive networking experience helped to build his confidence for when he met with the Principal of the College. He then made sure he maximized the opportunity to sell himself in the best light and in doing so unwittingly circumnavigated the main recruitment process, something which we will be covering in Chapter 4.

Build Your Confidence And Redesign Your Career

Understanding and managing your emotions during your career transition is key to your success. How well you do this, coupled with your attitude and approach to all the other aspects we have covered, will have a significant impact on how quickly you make your successful career change. There is a direct correlation between your confidence and your self-esteem when you eventually make a successful career change. Understanding this is very powerful and helps to build your momentum and shape your thinking about what will make the difference to keeping you moving towards your end goal.

Your confidence and how you are feeling about yourself and your situation will project very clearly through your body language, tone of voice, energy levels, how you communicate, as with Michael. So, please do yourself a favour and take heed of his insightful example.

A Golden Thread

You will find a number of true and inspiring case studies throughout this book, which are used to demonstrate an individual's success at each respective Step of the Cycle. The case studies will help you realise that you are not alone in facing the challenge of *winning through a career change* and that these role models, along with the rest of my book, may help to change your thinking and transform your life.

However, there is also a key story that demonstrates one person's transition through every Step of the Cycle that I will share with you at the end of each Chapter, together with a 'Pit Stop' to allow you to take time out and think about what had been achieved and how that might apply to you.

Mark my words, this is an interesting case study where the person made not one, but two winning career changes by the time he was just 30 years old and each time completely switched profession.

Each Step of the story has a clear 'Book Mark' to show you how far you are progressing one Step at a time. This unfolding story will let you discover that anything is possible with the right mindset, belief and positive actions.

Mark's Story

Step 1 – Let Go and Look Forward

Take your time, think, plan... and no more fire-fighting!

Mark encapsulates the essence of this Chapter in that he learnt to 'let go' and only then was able to begin to change. He knew when to walk away from a job and realise that age is not a barrier to your dreams.

After working for the same retailer for six years, Mark was stuck in a rut and at his first career crossroads. Retail work didn't pay well and he had personal goals he wanted to achieve, like getting on the property ladder. The unsociable shift patterns were at also odds with his active social life. When the company earmarked him for potential management roles, Mark felt it was time to walk away. One thing he definitely knew was that he didn't want a career in retail management!

Mark really wanted to work for the Fire Brigade. He was attracted to the physical side of the job and saw it as a respected career with potential for growth. He also thought his customer service skills would help. Over a period of three years he had applied numerous times for a position and even reached the final stages of the recruitment process. Despite his best efforts, it just wasn't working out for him, but rather than be beaten by circumstances there was the realisation that it was time to 'let go and look forward' and review career options.

But what to do next? Mark really wanted a physical job but he was at a loss as to how to progress. I started coaching him and challenged his thinking about what he really wanted from a job and to better understand the appeal of the Fire Brigade. I also encouraged him to share his situation and feelings with his friends - and very quickly one of his friends wanted to help. He told Mark about opportunities where he worked as a labourer for the 'Gas Emergency and Repair Services'. Mark quite liked the idea as he could see similarities with the Fire Brigade in view of the physical and emergency aspects required. Even better was the pay, flexible shifts and opportunities for progression. In light of Mark's enthusiasm and interest, his friend favourably mentioned him to his boss who subsequently asked Mark to submit his CV.

This presented another challenge for Mark's mindset, as he grew concerned that he felt he didn't have any relevant experience. Doubts began to surface: "Why would anyone want to employ me for such a job?" "How could I possibly make myself a strong candidate?"

My continued coaching allowed Mark to create a compelling CV and much to his surprise and delight, he was invited to interview. From Mark's physique it was evident that he could physically cope with the active demands of the role, so the issue was really about making the right impact at interview.

We worked together and prepared well by conducting a mock interview situation, practiced with possible model questions and developed his interview technique and behaviour. Mark then confidently went in to the interview and was over the moon to be told he had got the job. Mark had now positioned himself ready to move from retail and into a physically demanding manual job – his first major career change!

So how will Mark get on with his new challenge? Did he make the right CHOICE? Was he happy making that courageous switch?

...to be continued

PIT STOP
WINNING STEER

Mark is living proof that if you feel the time has come to walk away, you are probably right, even if letting go is difficult.

He overcame a lack of self-confidence and self-belief in making a career change by challenging the misperception of a lack of experience.

Shifting his mindset, securing the right support networks and having the courage to take positive action delivered positive results.

Persistence is known to pay-off but sometimes things happen for a reason – Mark knew when and what to quit to let go and move forward.

"Winners quit all the time.

They just quit the right stuff at the right time."

Seth Godin (US marketing guru and author), The Dip

Summary

- Your past does not equal nor does it dictate your future
- Consider your PERSPECTIVE
- If it is time for change then embrace it!
- Follow the *Do's* and be mindful of the *Don'ts* to manage the 'emotional roller coaster'
- Look at your personal development as a lifelong investment in your growth
- Your mindset really does matter!
- You are a work in progress and either *'Doing x and looking to change career to do work you love', or if returning to work you are 'in transition, exploring new opportunities'*
- Challenge your perceptions – are they real?
- You do have opportunity and CHOICE
- Learn to control your inner dialogue and self-talk
- Turn your FEAR into Focus
- Let your positive thoughts and feelings attract what you want
- Build your confidence to redesign your career
- Get the right support networks around you

- The Career Navigation Cycle process works -believe in it and take it step by step
- Acknowledge and celebrate your 'small wins'

Congratulations! You are now ready to move to the next step of the Cycle: **Re-evaluate.**

CHAPTER 2

It's Time To Re-evaluate – Step 2

"You spend more waking hours at work than in any other activity. Life is too short, so why be unhappy? Take the leap of faith and do what you love."

In this Chapter, we will explore Step 2 of the Cycle, which is key to any career change. Reflection, review and the output from challenging your thinking are the foundation you will build from. It is something you have probably rarely, if ever, done in any meaningful way. My experience is that most people view their careers and life as separate entities. It's when you start to re-evaluate that you realise your career and life are inextricably linked and you can lead a more fulfilling life by getting the balance right. The 'soul searching' exercises in this Chapter will help you with this re-evaluation. If you have not been in a job or career you love, then now is also the time to change your thinking and beliefs, so that your work becomes a key part of your life fulfilment.

Integral to this process is developing a good understanding of:

- What change **really means** to you
- What is important to you in your career and life and **why**
- The Importance of your Values and Needs
- How your financial situation can reshape your thinking
- Your vision of success

Many people want to start sending out CVs at this point, but as I have previously said, there is much work that needs to be done before you do that. **Please do not underestimate the importance and the immense benefit of this re-evaluation stage**. There will be a number of exercises to help you re-evaluate in a focused way. These will underpin much of your thinking and decision making as you move round the Cycle both now and for the rest of your career.

Navigate Your Way To A Brighter Future Toolkit

To help you work your way through the exercises, I have provided many additional resources, including bonus extras not featured in the book, on my website. These tools will add value to the book and are geared to help you work towards achieving your successful career transition or change. The toolkit contains:

- Free electronic worksheets for many of the key exercises in the book
- Free MP3 download -The first 30 minutes of my 'I Want A Career Change' 4CD/MP3 audio book set
- Free downloadable PDF with 5 pages of my Top Career Change Tips

You can download this toolkit of resources by registering at:

http://www.steveprestonthecareercatalyst.com

For some of the exercises, you may want to set up your own spreadsheets or create a table in Word (or similar).

With all of the exercises and key questions in this Chapter and the rest of the book, it is important that you are totally honest with yourself. There is no point in answering in any way other than being true to yourself.

This is the only way you will get authentic output that will enable you to follow through with the required positive action to achieve the outcomes you want.

All Change!

In this Chapter are some wonderful examples of clients and different people I have met who have had major 'eureka moments' when re-evaluating their careers and life situations. Moments which have prompted them to take drastic remedial action to transform their lives by changing careers.

By reading this book and working through the key exercises in this Chapter, you can plan your journey round the Cycle and be proactive too! First we will look at what will need to change in your career and life and most importantly **why**. This will set the scene before we explore what happens if you don't change and conversely from a positive mindset, what happens if you do.

What Needs To Change & WHY?

To get your career transition journey really moving, it is important to put some stakes in the ground to establish your current situation and find out where you are in various key aspects of your **career and life**. This will then help you to re-evaluate where you want to be and most importantly **why** and to prioritise what you want to address.

I often find that clients want to know 'what job or career they could change to or how they could change job or career' at this early stage. My answer is always the same, i.e. *"The **what** and **how** will come if you trust, believe and follow the career navigation Cycle process".* At this stage the most important aspect is **why** you want to change. The **why** is your purpose and if your **why** is strong enough, this will be your call to action and **what** you do and **how** you achieve your change will follow. Understanding **why** and your purpose will help you to take control of your career and 'become the architect of your own future'.

What Happens If You Don't Change?

Revisit the questions in the Introduction on *'How do you feel about your career'.* If you have never been fulfilled in your work, consider this excellent point which has been used by many famous thought leaders along the lines of *"If you always do what you've always done you will always get what you always got".* This surely sums up perfectly what happens if you don't change, doesn't it?

We have already looked at the importance of changing and moving with the times in Chapter 1. The longer you have been in a job, industry or particular sector, the harder making the break is likely to be. You may be afraid of making changes, but not changing will have far worse consequences, if you don't want *"what you always got".* Also, the longer you leave your decision to change, the more frustrated you will become and this will impact on your life and those around you, especially your nearest and dearest at just the time you want their empathy and support.

I'm sure you don't want any of these statements to be what becomes of you do you?

- You never realise your true potential
- You constantly wonder 'what if'
- You become ever more frustrated and unhappy
- You settle for a life of compromise
- You never challenge yourself
- You accept your work is a means to an end
- You become a 'wage slave'

The reality is that when you are unhappy in your work it can have many repercussions with the most severe affecting:

- Your health
- Your relationships
- Your social life
- Your outlook on life

What Happens If You Do Change?

Let's now look at the positive things that can happen when you do make changes, as the following case study illustrates. It's a wonderful example of accepting that change must happen, taking control of your career and taking positive action by investing in yourself and your future.

Sam's Story

A few years ago, I ran my *'Navigate the Way to a Brighter Future'* seminar at the 'One Life Live' exhibition at Olympia in London. Like this book, the seminar, was about how to make a successful career change. We had an audience of around two hundred people with some people dropping by our stand afterwards to see us and chat. Sam told us how much she had enjoyed the seminar and asked for more information about our career development programmes. She was on the phone to me first thing the next morning asking me if I minded that she had phoned me before I got round to calling her. Goodness me if only all potential clients were that proactive!

She cut to the chase quickly telling me that a comment I made in the seminar had been going round in her head all weekend. I had said, rather tongue in cheek, something along the lines of "As much as we like seeing you at the exhibition, we don't want to see you again next year, unless it is to share your success." This had resonated strongly with Sam as, in her own words, "If I come back again next year and nothing has changed, I will have failed!"

Sam was definitely at a career crossroads. She had spent twenty years developing her career with a major plc.

She had a good middle management role but by her own admission had lost her way and she no longer shared the values and ethos of the company, which had changed radically. My warning was her call to action and despite her difficult financial situation, she decided it was time to move on and invest in herself and her career for the first time in her life. This begs the question of how few people ever invest in themselves. You may spend money sending your kids to university or have a portfolio of financial investments but you are in the minority if you have ever invested in your own career and personal development. When the benefits can be so significant and life changing, this is crazy, isn't it?

From a standing start, Sam worked her way through my Breakthrough Career Development programme, round the entire Career Navigation Cycle and made a career change in less than three months! Her turning point was the realisation that it was time for her to make changes in her life and take positive action, rather than procrastinating as she had been doing for years. I was so impressed with Sam, especially for her natural coaching and training skills, which we discovered through the coaching. With her enthusiasm, energy and determination, I felt she would make a great coach and trainer herself, which is exactly what happened. Sam became a key part of my associate team on a major project. In no time at all she was getting rave reviews from her clients, gained a coaching qualification with the result that her self-confidence soared, she was fulfilled and she has since moved on with both her career and life.

As I discussed in Chapter 1, you can resist change or you can see it as an opportunity. In this Chapter, you will find that change is also a chance to re-evaluate yourself and your life to see if you want to do things differently and reap the rewards, just as Sam did. There are a number of ways of identifying the areas of your life you want to change, which we will explore. As with Sam, the best results come once you accept you must change. You can then take control of your **life and career** to take the positive action to become the architect of your own future. Your next step:

Stock Take

What Is Important To You In Your Career & Life & WHY

In our fast moving world and lives, most people rarely stop and reflect. Instead they tend to stumble through life. Does this sound familiar? Most importantly, if you are looking to change career, you now have a great opportunity to take stock, put some new stakes in the ground and re-evaluate some key areas of your life. You may even decide o take some time out at this stage, but consider carefully the implications of this which we will look at shortly.

What better time than now to start focusing on getting your life and career into balance and working towards finding a job, career or work you love and creating the life you want? This leads nicely into our first main exercise, *'The Wheel of Life'*. This exercise will help you take a holistic view of your life to establish how balanced your life is and focus your energy on the key areas you wish to improve moving forward. This is an excellent way to kick start your re-evaluation process. The next section will guide you through how to use the exercise for maximum benefit.

✎ *Exercise - The Wheel of Life: Are You Happy With Your Life & Is It In Balance?*

The Wheel of Life is used in many coaching situations because it is an excellent foundation to build on, when looking at making changes in your life, so this is a great start point for your re-evaluation of your career and life. You will find other examples of the Wheel of Life. I have adapted this version based on many years of experience working with different types of clients to include what I believe to be the most relevant categories for people working through career change. The exercise may trigger thinking around similar categories you also wish to focus on, which is fine. Otherwise, just work and focus on the categories I have listed.

The Wheel of Life: How balanced is my life?

The Wheel of Life has 8 categories	My Score
Fun - Happiness, Hobbies, Leisure	
Relationship - Current or Future Life Partner	
Career - Job satisfaction, Career path	
Family - Children, Parents, Relatives	
Social - Friends, Sport, Activities	
Health - Exercise, Diet, Well-Being	
Financial - Savings, Investments	
Creative - Self-space, Personal Growth, Spiritual, Artistic	

- Assign a number from 1 to 10 next to each category. Write 1 in the second column if you are very unsatisfied in this area and up to 10 if you are totally satisfied.

- Look at the picture of the circle on the next page. Thinking of the outside of the circle as 10 and the centre as 1, draw a line in each segment to represent your score. You can see a completed example at the bottom of the next page
- Join up the lines between each segment. This represents the balance in your life!
- Look at your scores - What are the 2 lowest scores?
- What are the 2 areas that you would most like to move forward?

Moving forward:

1. How would you feel if you could significantly move forward in these 2 areas?
2. Action - What could you do now to start moving forward in these areas?

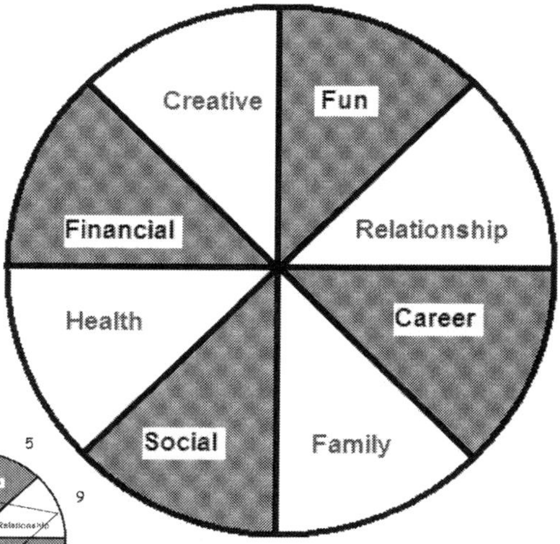

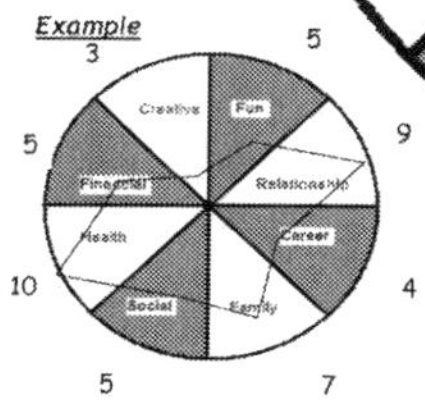

How does your Wheel look?

I can guarantee it is unlikely your wheel of life will be a complete circle, unless the circle has mid to low scores on each segment. The majority of people have a wheel somewhat similar to what you might see on the Flintstones, so don't worry if this is how yours looks as it can only get better from now on. If you, like the majority of my clients, have never seen this exercise previously, you are starting to unravel some brilliant new insights. You may for the first time start to see why you have felt unhappy. Regardless, you can now proactively manage your life to ensure you achieve the right balance for you.

This is just the start of your 'voyage of self-discovery.' Importantly, now that you have committed in writing to your focus, you have started making a plan to take action and you are doing something positive about the aspects of your life you want to change. This is a key step in the change process and what gets measured gets done!

How Important Is It To Love Your Job Or The Work You Do?

Confucius, Chinese Teacher, Editor, Politician, and Philosopher (551BC - 479BC) says *"Choose a job you love and you will never work a day in your life".*

What a wonderful fulfilling statement. You may have never considered how important it is to love what you do. Now you are re-evaluating what is important to you in your career and life and **why**, you have reason to do so. Everyone will have a different take on this. However, if you look at people who really do love what they do, most of them are more energised and **they don't even view what they do as work**. Now is your opportunity to work towards achieving this same goal. How good would that feel? Great, I'm sure!

Sir David Attenborough the naturalist and broadcaster, is an extreme but brilliant example. A remarkable man, now in his 90's and still working hard, including all sorts of challenging expeditions for TV shows and enjoying life. Why? Because he is passionate about his work and the Planet! I'm sure you know people like this and they are a joy to be around. This is why I developed my 'mantra', *"You spend more waking hours at work than in any other activity. Life is too short, so why be unhappy? Take the leap of faith and do what you love."*

Some of my clients say *"I don't believe you can actually find work you love. How do people actually end up loving what they do?"* There is no magic wand; there is no 'holy grail'. You need to work through the process, which most people will never do. The answers will eventually evolve from reading this book and following my Career Navigation Cycle process. The following case study highlights vividly what can happen if your life is out of balance and equally what can happen when it is in balance. You now have the opportunity to proactively manage your career to become the architect of your own future and create the life you want. I'm sure you'll agree this sounds appealing, doesn't it?

Boyd Lemon's Story

I came across Boyd on the business social networking site, LinkedIn (I will be making more key references to the importance of Social Media and LinkedIn in Chapter 4); where I was involved in discussions about the importance of doing what you love. Boyd had made some interesting comments in relation to his life story, so I asked him to provide a short overview for this book. He happily did this and it makes powerful reading:

"As a young man, just out of law school, working for a prestigious Los Angeles law firm, my focus was on doing the best job I could to reach the ultimate achievement - becoming a partner of the law firm. I was married and at the age of 27 became a father, but I relegated my family to second place in my priorities. I was so focused on my work that I ignored my family, particularly my wife's needs, without realising it. From time to time doubts about whether practicing law, helping the rich to get richer, was what I wanted to be doing, but I pushed those doubts down to the bottom of my consciousness by working hard and using alcohol to numb my consciousness when I wasn't working. Eventually my wife left me. I repeated the same scenario with wives two and three and found myself, at the age of 56, single, still practicing law and abusing alcohol. I began to scratch the surface of my melancholy".

"At 63 I met two young women who helped me break through, both artists, one a dancer, the other a song writer. They became my best friends without any romantic ties. I made plans to retire from the practice of law and one evening I mentioned to the song writer that I would like to write fiction. In two years I wrote about 15 short stories. I loved writing and I finally had found my calling. Doing what you love, probably the single most important thing in life. I didn't understand this for most of my adulthood, but, at least, I finally figured it out."

Boyd focused his first book on his failed marriages and what he learnt about himself through his journey. He published "Digging Deep: A Writer Uncovers His Marriages (2011)" and has since published more books, overcome his alcohol problem and is living proof you are never too old to change your career.

Don't be like Boyd and leave it so late in life to change and do what you love. Why waste so much of your life being unhappy or unfulfilled? Just think what sort of life Boyd might have had if he had listened to his 'inner voice' about his doubts around his legal career?

What he experienced at this early stage of his career was a challenge to his Values and Needs. We will explore the importance of being true to these later in this Chapter.

Fulfilment Or 'Wage Slave'?

As I mentioned right at the start of this book, research over the last decade consistently shows that 1 in 2 people are in 'the wrong job' and 2 out of 3 are 'unfulfilled'. This is startling to say the least and such people are effectively 'wage slaves'. We all know people who feel this way about their jobs, who spend their lives moaning and groaning about their company, boss etc. You may also feel this way right now?

Many people inadvertently fall into a job or career, me included. It may not have been part of a master plan but more likely a result of advice you were given, a contact you knew or even family connections getting you started. You may have stayed in the same sector for many years, even if you have changed jobs a few times, perhaps taking on new roles but remaining in your comfort zone and commanding an increasingly good salary. However, there often comes a point when you get stale, there is a major reorganisation, big management or culture change, or you no longer feel in tune with the values of the organisation, which then challenges the way you feel about your job or career.

The good news is that, regardless of your situation, you can start to do something positive about your situation now. Life is too short to be forever thinking about 'what if's' so grasp the opportunity and work towards finding the job, career or work you really want and love, so you start looking forward to getting out of bed each day with a real sense of purpose.

The 'Velvet Rut'

A most interesting spin on fulfilment versus 'wage slave' came from a fascinating client, Mary, who coined the phrase the '*Velvet Rut*.' I had never heard of this before but it's a classic description to exemplify how, if you are commanding top packages (she was a City Trader), you get stuck in this awful rut and metaphorical tug of war. On one hand you have a high salary and fantastic bonuses but on the other, you may absolutely hate what you do. The trappings and the lifestyle are what keep you there as it becomes a hard wrench to leave them behind. For many people this is also about ego and 'one-upmanship' over your friends and peers. Only when something happens to suddenly awaken the senses do you realise that this is really not what you want out of life (in most cases it's usually burn out). It makes you sit up, take notice and start to take stock.

I have worked with many people in this situation where it has become blatantly obvious that in most of the areas in their lives they are extremely unhappy and must make changes, but they have to battle against the trappings of 'the velvet rut'. The majority eventually took brave decisions to break out and change their lives. We will come back to Mary later in the Chapter after we look at Values and Needs.

"Success is a journey not a destination"

Ben Sweetland, Author and Psychologist

What Does Success Mean To You?

We have explored how unhappy we can become when stuck in unfulfilling jobs, yet what fulfils us at work and in our lives and to what extent we live to work is so different for each of us. Have you ever really thought about your vision of success? Is it about money and material wealth, travel, a balanced lifestyle, health and happiness or a combination of all these? The Wheel of Life exercise and the Values and Needs exercise, in this Chapter, may also give you some inspiration for your vision of success, so you can start work on your journey.

✎ *Exercise – What Is Your Vision Of Success?*

You are probably starting to get a picture of many things you don't want out of life but let's now consider what you really **do want out** of life. What does success mean to you in terms of your work and personal life, as it is important that you have a vision of success to aspire to? The Wheel of Life exercise is an excellent start point but the aim here is for you to 'dig deep' and consider what does success mean for you? *What do you see and feel? As you begin to consider this statement now, what can you visualise and what sort of feeling or emotion does that create?*

To aid your thinking, here are three key questions for you to consider:

- What do you want to be?
- What do you want to do?
- What do you want to have?

These three aspects are key principles in the Law of Attraction and by focusing your thoughts and feelings on your vision, it can help you manifest and attract the right people, work, opportunities etc.

You can do this in a number of ways:

- Draw a picture on a large sheet of paper that represents your vision of success.

- Make a collage by cutting out pictures from magazines to build up a picture of what success looks like to you.
- Create using an online vision board. There are now many of these excellent resources readily available at no cost or low cost on the web.
- Write a short story about your vision or even 'A Successful Day in your Life'.

It is important not to hold back when doing this exercise. You are envisioning the creation of your own wonderful future. This is your vision and therefore nothing is out of bounds, as anything is possible with the right mindset, belief and positive actions, so dream away!

Once you have done this exercise it is worth pinning up your vision board, drawing or story somewhere in your house, phone or tablet, so that you can see it every day. Taking this approach has worked really well for some of my most successful clients, as the constant reminder of your vision of success will be implanted into your unconscious mind and will spur you on to achieve your dream or goals. Give this exercise your best shot.

You can always revisit it as you progress through the book and gain new ideas and inspiration flashes through your mind!

What Gets You Out Of Bed Each Day?

No not that old joke about your alarm clock or Smartphone! Having done some stock taking, you are now starting to gain real insight into what is important to you in your career and life and why. Digging deeper, we now want to consider some of your key motivators and drivers, as this will give you even more powerful information to help you re-evaluate. Let's now look at your must have Values and Needs in your career and life because this will provide some real clues as to:

- Why you want to work
- What really gets you out of bed each day

Understanding Your Values & Needs

"Success goes where your energy flows."

We all have a set of values; they are the things we believe in and hold dear. They often change over time. We are unlikely to have exactly the same values as an adult that we had as a teenager, but we rarely audit or even consider them. We also have a set of needs. These are things that we must have in order to feel motivated and they contribute to our overall sense of wellbeing. Without understanding your values and needs it is almost impossible to find real meaning and fulfilment, which is fundamental when it comes to finding the right work for you. You need to establish:

- What motivates you?
- What drives you?
- What you want to take forward with you in the future?

You rarely consider your Values and Needs until you are facing a significant event or change of circumstances in your life, such as marriage, divorce, parenthood, an organisational restructure where you may be displaced, or the realisation that you are so fed up with your job that you want to walk away and start all over again. Values and Needs are things we probably take for granted. In my case it was really brought home to me big time after the death of my Father. At that time

I was considering rekindling my executive career. Suddenly this felt hugely insignificant, as there were far more important things in life, not least how on earth my Mother would cope without him, as they had been 'joined at the hip' for over fifty years. I realised that having more flexibility was something I now valued and needed.

When I was working in the corporate world, one of my ambitions was to retire at 55. I thought by then I would have done enough and would want to slow down. I had visions of spending my time doing things I enjoy, like more time to play golf, more time with my wife, taking more holidays and the other things you rarely get the chance to do when you are working full on for an employer. Since doing what I love, in the career coaching world, writing, speaking and running my business, retirement couldn't be further from my mind. I am now past the magic 55 and want to carry on working for as long as I feel I'm enjoying it. My ultimate reward is making a difference to the lives of other people by helping them to transform their careers and lives. There is no better feeling for me and this is what drives me. I guarantee that whatever career plan you've set, once you change career and start doing something you love, your whole perspective will change and how good would that feel?

Let's now assess your own Values and Needs with this simple but effective exercise:

Exercise - Values And Needs - Getting To Know You

The table below shows some of the most common or important Values and Needs, which will ultimately help you to consider what you want out of a future job, career or working lifestyle. You will also find a more challenging, powerful and empowering online version of this exercise on my website via this link:

http://www.steveprestonthecareercatalyst.com/product/career-values/

Show **CVN10** in the Coupon box **to save £10.**

So, what do you want from a future job or working lifestyle?

Example: if you think *freedom to make my own decisions* is really important, you would tick this in the Essential column. Likewise, if *long term security and stability* is no longer important, as let's face it how can you guarantee this anymore, you would tick the Not Important column and so on.

		Essential	Desirable	Not Important
AUTONOMY	Freedom to make my own decisions			
	Working autonomously			
	Freedom from organisational rules and constraints			
	Ability to define my own tasks, schedules and procedures			

STABILITY & SECURITY	A clearly mapped out career path			
	Job that requires steady, predictable performance			
	Long term security and stability			
	Working in a stable, well-known organisation			
	Incremental pay and benefits based on length of service			
ENTERPRISE	Creating new organisations, products and services			
	Building my own business			
	Owning something developed from my ideas and efforts			
	Producing things that people associate with me			
	Showing people I can build a fortune			
	Being able to take risks			

SENSE OF PURPOSE	Providing a service to help others			
	Contributing to the wider community			
	Dedication to a particular course			
	Having a job of real value			
	Making a difference in the world			
BALANCED LIFESTYLE	A balanced personal and professional lifestyle			
	Flexible working hours and practices (able to work at home)			
	Relatively low levels of geographical movement			
	Sufficient time for pastimes, holidays and relaxing			

EXPERTISE & CHALLENGE	Developing a specialism to a high level of excellence			
	Being recognised as an expert in the field			
	Ability to use my special skills and talents			
	Solving complex problems			
	Regular challenges to stretch my abilities and skills			
REWARD & RECOGNITION	Having a good standard of living			
	Being recognised for my achievements			
	Having a well paid job			
	Being highly regarded by others			
	Reaching a respected social status			

AUTHORITY & INFLUENCE	Responsibility for making decisions			
	Advancement up the organisational ladder			
	Ability to influence, supervise, lead and control people			
	Contributing to the success of my organisation			
	Accountability for finances and resources			
GENERAL	Variety			
	Physical challenge - you enjoy doing something that is physically demanding			
	Working with others, in a team			
	Contact with people			
	Creativity - thinking up new ideas and ways of doing things			
	Working alone			

GENERAL	Place of work - it is important that you work in the right part of the country for you			
	Competition- you enjoy competing against other people or groups			
	You like working to deadlines			
	Communication - being able to express ideas well in writing and speech			
	Precise work which involves great care and concentration			
	Peace - to have few pressures or uncomfortable demands			
	Artistic - work involving drawing, designing, making music, making models			
	Having close friendships at work			
	Excitement in your work			
	The opportunity to learn new things			

Next Steps

- Taking your **'Essential'** category only, select your **top ten** values and needs
- Now **prioritise these with one being the most important** and **ten the least important**
- The aim is to get a **focused top ten** that you feel is a true representation of what you value and need most from a future job or work
- You can also **map your top ten Values and Needs against your present or most recent jobs** and this will help to explain why you enjoyed some more than others
- You now have powerful information you can use to establish if any jobs you might be considering are right for you, whether you need to rethink or if self-employment is an option

What Are Your Values & Needs Telling You?

Are there any surprises?

Look closely, as you may well find clues emerging that you might not have previously considered. Keep an open mind and you never know what opportunities may appear. For example, you may now feel that *contributing to the wider community* is something you would highly value. If so, this could open up a whole new world of thinking around the type of job, organisation, sector or even a business you could start of your own. This is highly individual, so there is no right or wrong. What is important is what feels right for you, looking forward to your *'brighter future'*.

PIT STOP WINNING STEER

Back to Mary, she was a classic example of someone whose Values were completely at odds with both the organisation she worked for and the type of work she was doing. It got so bad that one day she just decided she'd had enough and walked out! Mary was then committed to following her dream - she wanted to be a paramedic.

By following the Cycle process, she ultimately achieved her ambition, despite having to overcome many challenges around her fears and limiting beliefs, which you may also have to face at various stages along the way. Mary did and won through, so you can too!

Mary proved that if your Values are at odds with the organisation and what you want to achieve in your life and all the other key strands of your life aren't working, then you must address these particular areas before the consequences are too great.

Mary has since relocated, changed her career again, moved into a frontline role in a hospital and also got married! Mary has shown what can happen when you get your life in balance, understand your Values and Needs and live your life by them.

How To Work In The Future - Introducing Portfolio Careers and the 3 Ps

As you can see, when you start to re-evaluate things, it can open up a new world of possibilities. Some of my clients looking to change careers find a completely different type of job or set up their own business. Also, many of them have chosen to develop a 'portfolio career'. We will cover portfolio careers again in Chapters 3 and 4 in particular, as the appeal for such an approach often increases after you have completed Step 3 of the Cycle **(Establishing Your True Marketability)** after which you may decide to seriously consider a portfolio career during Step 4 (exploring opportunities).

Essentially, a portfolio career is about changing your mindset from having 'a job' to deriving income from a number of different sources. You can earn from using any combination of activities, interests, skills, talents and passions to create the working lifestyle you want. **This is what I call *'working for Passion, Pleasure and Profit'* or now to be referred to as the 3 Ps.** How good does this sound?

- A part-time employed job and your own business
- Two or three part-time jobs, similar or different
- A part-time job or your own business and voluntary work
- Regular interim or freelance projects alongside other occasional work (we will cover these options in Chapter 5)
- Being your own boss but having different strands to your business or even having different businesses
- A full-time employed job and developing your business alongside this

As we go through the book I will give examples of clients and other people I know who have interesting and fulfilling portfolio.

Careers based around the 3 Ps. To whet your appetite let's take a look at my best mate Don, who since I first wrote this has tragically passed on:

Don's Story

Don was a gardener, trainer, career adviser, outplacement consultant, CV writer and a magician! After many years working in different sales and management roles, Don took the option of redundancy, which happened unexpectedly. He wasn't keen on commuting and decided it was time to get out of the corporate rat race but what to do next? Don discussed his thinking with his wife and mostly with me over a beer in our local pub, which is always a useful refuge for creative thinking! He decided it was time to change career, work locally and do something he really loved.

After doing his survival budget (see next section) Don decided to start up his own gardening business, which was a real passion. Eventually, he developed a portfolio career using a number of other skills and interests. Within a short period of time he added training to the mix (he was a qualified trainer from his previous role) and over time, I networked him into Career Advice & Guidance and the whole Career Development field. Don then added another lifelong interest and passion and turned his love of magic (previously just a hobby) into another income stream.

On one amazing day, a few summers ago, Don did gardening in the morning, ran our career transition workshop in the afternoon and finished the day with a magic show for a local society in the evening. He was absolutely buzzing the next morning! What a different way to earn a living by doing all the things you love?

I should point out that Don never worked excessive hours but chose how and when he worked, ensuring he maintained a good work-life balance. Most interestingly, having known Don for many years, I never envisaged him running his own business. I am convinced this was never on his radar until he had to re-evaluate his options. Twenty years later Don was still self-employed and even turned down a number of highly paid jobs during this period. Why? Because for Don, like many of my clients and people I know, when they take stock and re-evaluate, it wasn't about earning loads of money but 'earning enough'. What was much more important was his portfolio career, which offered him the choice, variety and flexibility he valued most. **What a brilliant example of working for the 3 Ps!**

Reassess & Rethink Your Finances

Whatever your reason for considering changing careers, if you are unsure what to do next then understanding and re-evaluating your finances are of the utmost importance. Let's get started, as by doing this exercise thoroughly it can help you focus your mind and open up new thinking in ways you may not have considered previously.

What Do You Need To Live On?

Pension

If you have had a relatively long career and paid into company pension schemes for a number of years, unless the majority of your pension is held in a public sector scheme, I would highly recommend getting an independent review. When you are in the cut and thrust of daily working life, you may take just a cursory glance at your annual pension statement. Don't assume your pension is working well for you. Despite thirty years of contributions, my pension was going significantly backwards, due to market conditions and poor investments from the trustees. I contacted a friend, who is an Independent Financial Adviser, and I owe him a huge debt, as he helped to redress my underperforming pension and we now review the performance at least once a year. You don't want to be in the same position as I was, do you? If you are in a company pension scheme and your employer does not provide a pension review as part of your exit, I recommend you take this action yourself, sooner rather than later.

✎ *Exercise - Survival Budget*

The *Survival Budget* is a key tool and another very powerful and important exercise for anyone at a career crossroads, in transition, regardless of your situation. Whether you are planning to start your own business or considering any other type of career change, re-evaluating your finances is key. Knowing how much you need to earn as against how much you want to earn, or how much you have earned in the past is an invaluable exercise. Why?... Because quite simply this becomes the yardstick you can use to focus your mind on what might be possible, moving forward. For many people, like me, this exercise has helped to open up a whole new world of possibilities!

For example:

You may have had a brilliant career and be earning a six-figure or serious executive salary but have had enough of the corporate world or working at an executive level in the public services and have decided that you want to get out of the 'rat race'. It is highly likely you will be earning less when you first make your change, especially if you start up your own business. By doing your sums, you can see very easily how much you need to earn, which is a great start point, don't you think?

For the majority of people, the older you are the less your outgoings become, especially once any children have flown the nest. Therefore, if you've had a good or long career your survival budget can often be a pleasant surprise. For younger people, if you have a high mortgage or family overheads, it could be harder to make that change into work you would really love to do. You may need to make some major sacrifices or compromises. This doesn't mean to say you cannot achieve your desired goal for a career change but you may need to consider whether this becomes an immediate goal or longer term goal instead, while you work towards this alongside another job. Ultimately, if you are seeking fulfilment, you don't want to let your financial situation hold you back, as I'm sure you don't want to be thinking *'what if'*, for years to come do you?

Note: This is a personal survival budget not a business one. If you decide to start up your own business you will need to add in various start up and running costs, which you will need to research. We will review self-employment and starting a business in more detail in Chapter 5.

Complete the following table of income and outgoings. Your total survival budget equals your income minus your outgoings.

Monthly income		**Monthly outgoings**	
Partner salary/ income.		Mortgage or rent.	
Other income e.g. rent from working children.		House – insurances plus general maintenances.	
Interest from savings.		Car/s - mot, tax, insurance plus running costs including petrol.	
Dividends from shares and other investments.		Utilities – electric, gas, phone, mobile, broadband, TV etc.	
Tax credits if applicable.		Food – typical weekly shop.	
Child Benefit.		Holidays – budget for what you typically spend.	

Pension (if able to draw some/all).		Leisure – watching and playing sport, gym membership, hobbies, music, cinema.	
Other income.		Social – Meals out, entertaining, pub.	
Lump sum compromise or redundancy package (if applicable) broken into 12 monthly chunks.		Children – pocket money, schooling, clothes, entertaining, trips, and school holiday clubs. If older then university costs.	
		Clothes for you and your partner.	
		Grooming – hairdressing, make up and accessories.	
		Birthdays, Christmas.	
		Pets – food, insurance, upkeep etc.	
		Subscriptions – magazines, trade publications.	
		Contingencies.	
		Other outgoings:	
Total income		**Total outgoings**	
	Total Survival Budget		

Note: this will be net of tax, so you need to add a minimum of 20% on top to allow for this

Having completed your budget, you can now work out how much you need to earn in order to survive. Here is an example: if your annual income is £30,000 without your salary and your outgoings total £50,000 you will need to earn £20,000 net of tax yourself in order to balance your household outgoings to survive. At the current UK tax band rates this would equate to around £25,000 gross salary or self-employed income. Much will depend on what other allowances you are entitled to. To be totally sure you would need to check with HMRC (https://www.gov.uk/browse/tax/income-tax) to establish your situation. If you are living outside the UK then you would need to check with your respective government tax department.

Now that you have identified your incomings and outgoings, you might also need to consider working out how long your savings will last if you decide to take time out for a while, to work at your career change, or if you are starting a business from scratch. It will definitely pay you to get some impartial financial advice to review how best to invest your money or any inheritance you might be about to receive. This will help you create the life you want now and in the longer term.

Malcolm's Story - Shaking off the shackles of corporate boardroom life

"I was a plc board director who was 'very bored' with big company politics. I had wanted to go it alone for years but lacked the courage. Then one day I was holed up at home with the flu and for once had time to think about my future. I decided that now was the time to be bold and set about calculating all my worldly goods, investments, savings etc.

I determined that if I started my business venture and it didn't work out, I would still be able to support my young family; we would just have to move to a smaller house. This was all the reassurance I needed to take the leap of faith that I had previously not been brave enough to take. I resigned my position 3 days later when I returned to work. That was 15 years ago. Regrets? None - except I should have done it sooner!"

Malcolm's story demonstrates the real benefit of doing your survival budget. It literally provides you with the evidence you need to make your decision. This is what other clients have said over the years, having worked out their survival budgets:

'Maybe I could get a part-time job while I develop my business to help pay the bills'

'I can still do the voluntary work I enjoy outside of work as long as I cover my living costs'

'I will get another full-time job and develop my business idea at my own pace'

'I don't need to work at the same level again so could consider doing a less stressful job, just working part-time and spending more time on my hobbies or developing a portfolio career'

Survival Tips

1. Allow for 'desirables'

- From my own experience, it is good to build in 'desirables' as you still need to live.
- This is especially true if you have children who might not understand why all of a sudden they can't do the things

they have been used to, if you are taking time out while making your career change.

- Also what is the point of making unnecessary changes to your lifestyle, if this is an important part of your general well-being and happiness?

2. See where you can make savings?

- Use your list of outgoings to help you trim excessive or unnecessary costs to save money.
- Have a close look at your phone, TV and broadband packages, all your insurance policies, gym membership etc. to see if you are able to get a better deal, which can then pay for a nice treat at some point.
- Unless you always vigilantly monitor and manage your finances on a regular basis, you will be amazed at where you can make savings. See what you can trim back that you won't miss or where you can make immediate cost savings, especially by renegotiating your current arrangements.

3. Don't skimp unless you have to

- I have come across many people who go through the survival budget process and while in transition, decide to cut everything to the bone and as a result don't go out and avoid spending money at all costs!
- Unless your finances are in dire straits, it is important not to 'become an island', as I mentioned in Chapter 1.
- Your career transition is a time when you need to meet people to build and develop relationships and new networks. This need not cost you lots of money, just the occasional coffee, beer or glass of wine. However, if you are really strapped, get the other people to pay and

make sure you return the favour when you have made a successful change.

4. Build in contingencies

- Always allow for the unexpected e.g. repairs to your car, work on the house or electrical items needing replacement.

5. Worst case scenario

- If you have taken time out to make your change, how long will your money last and what would happen if your money ran out?
- What would your options be? For example:
- You could look for temporary work or an interim contract rather than a new full-time role for immediacy of work.
- Alternatively, if you have a partner who is not working would it be more beneficial for them to find work if they can command a higher salary and you swap household roles? I have a number of clients who have done this.
- If you decide to start a business, it may be helpful for your partner to secure a better paid job or even part-time work whilst you are getting established to cover your bills.

6. Taking remedial action

- If your situation is such that your money will soon run out, there is still positive action you can take, to salvage your situation, whilst you decide what your next step will be.
- I know a number of people, who decided to rent out a spare room in their house for a period of time to give them breathing space, while they made their career transition,

set up a business or were growing their business to the next level. This can often work well to give you time while you get back on your feet again. Also, if you live alone, this can help to offset the isolation.

- In extreme cases, where you need to take drastic action in order to fund a business or you wish to have an easier life in the twilight years of your career, you always have the option to downsize your property to free up some cash.

If you follow through with the principles and the guidelines in this book, you stand a much better chance of not needing to take such radical action. However, being aware of the options will focus your mind on the final deadline by which you need to achieve your end goal and successful career transition.

7. Continue the discipline

- Once you have developed your survival budget, this is an excellent discipline to continue. It becomes a constantly evolving project as and when your circumstances change e.g. kids leaving home, going to university, your partner changing jobs, you getting a better or lesser paid job, moving house or your business really taking off. You now have a readymade tool to help you budget.

What would you be reluctant to give up?

Both my wife and I have a background in the travel industry, so holidays have always been important to us and an integral part of our life and budget. When I was in transition, we still had holidays but toned them down until I was earning well again. Now our children are independent, we only need to budget for the two of us, but our aim is to have a break of some kind every 3 to 4 months to keep us fresh and always have something to look forward to. Holidays are a big chunk of our annual survival budget but equally a key part of our 'life plan', taking priority over other desirables. Likewise consider what you will be reluctant to give up?

How has your survival budget affected your thinking?

Having completed this exercise you may have identified areas where you can start saving or you have found you don't need to earn as much as you thought. This can be extremely liberating, which can open up completely new thinking, as was the case for me.

When I realised how much I needed to earn versus what I had been earning, I felt confident that I would be able to generate this income from running my own business, given all the skills, attributes and knowledge I had developed over the years.

Although I did not know what I wanted to do at this stage, it was hugely reassuring to know I would only need to earn around half of my previous salary, so starting a business suddenly felt very achievable. Although you may not have considered self-employment, starting your own business or even a portfolio career, what would a similar scenario mean for you?

Paul's Story

An excellent example which helps to encapsulate much of the learning from this Chapter is Paul, a top strategic IT Consultant, who told me his story:

"My moment of truth came to me when I was 30,000 feet in the air. I was heading across the Atlantic to America in mid-July having traveled 60,000 air miles that year. I had a loving partner and two boys now entering their teenage years. It dawned on me that I was literally travelling the wrong way (in so many ways). My career progression was in control of me rather than the other way around. At risk was the loss of a loving family, which felt unacceptable. I put away my ego and fear.

The solution was radical. With no plans for the future I resigned and was gone within a month. I took the family on holiday for the summer and started to build relationships with the people that really mattered to me. My boss thought me completely mad! However six months later I had set up a consultancy and won contracts. I was earning more than when I had travelled the world as a senior employee. I was in control of my career and never looked back. Today I have what many people spend most of their lives looking for: CHOICE!

I can work on things that I find motivating; it just so happens that I also make good money and every day is interesting. My best friends are my family and I go to sleep each night contented and thank my god for giving me a good kicking at 30,000 feet! One year after I had resigned I heard that 8,000 jobs were lost at the company I had worked for, including the boss who thought me mad. In fact, my function was completely cut, so where would I be now?"

What can we learn from Pauls' story?

The majority of these learning points can be found in the Summary below. Another key point is, if you have been neglecting your partner or family, this could be a great time to bring you closer by taking a complete break, if your finances allow for this. By doing so, this will clearly give you some breathing space to re-evaluate your career and life. If you do decide to start your own business, the break will be viewed positively by potential clients as doing proper research, business planning and getting 'your ducks in a row', will all help you to start on the right footing.

- Reassess your finances to understand how much you need to earn to reframe your thinking
- Put the survival tips into practice and continue the disciplines
- You may not want a traditional job any longer, if so an option is to consider a portfolio career
- Understand the importance of your Values and Needs and what gets you out of bed each day
- What is your vision of success? Dream it, feel it, see it, display it so you can make it happen
- Think about what happens if you don't change and imagine how you will feel if you do!
- You may not want a traditional job any longer; if so an option is to consider a portfolio career **and working for the 3 Ps, Passion, Pleasure and Profit!**

Mark's Story (continued)

2

Step 2 – It's Time To Re-evaluate

When your values are compromised.

Having won through his first career change from retail into a manual job, Mark thrived on the physical demands of the job and the responsibility – he was very happy.

However, during the recession the company was acquired by a much larger organisation. The previous culture of support and engagement was replaced by one of micromanagement, bullying and nepotism. Mark was also concerned that safety was being compromised due to the added pressure of the need to get jobs done quickly. Nonetheless, he battled on and was eventually promised a promotion, only to find that the decision was unprofessionally rescinded. Company morale sank to an all-time low, the workplace had become 'toxic' and Mark's previously good health was suffering. Even though he had previously made a successful career change, Mark was in the fog and struggling to see the wood for the trees. The same question from Step 1 began to surface again... But what to do next? How could Mark now move away from such a physical role for something different?

My Career Navigation Cycle resonated with Mark as he embraced this next step to take stock of the situation and re-evaluate what he wanted from his career and life and why. His values were important but these were now beginning to conflict with the changing organisation. Committed to a mortgage, finances were a key issue... so what would be the next step and would Mark have the resilience to see it through?

...to be continued

- As part of his re-evaluation, Mark had to take a step back and 'let go' of a number of aspects, before he could move forward
- It is not uncommon to move back and forth between the different Steps of the Cycle as you respond to changing circumstances
- The acquisition of the company, unexpected new ownership and change of culture clashed with his values
- Overcoming a perceived 'guilt' of walking away from a specialist role he had trained for over a period of years to have become an expert

- Was it possible to command another similarly high salary by relinquishing those additional paid allowances for work of a dangerous nature, shifts and being 'on call'?
- The possible loss of a good work-life balance which enabled him to work shifts and plan free time for the gym and a good social life

Summary

I trust that some of the inspiring stories in this Chapter will make you sit up, want to re-evaluate and to take control of your career to become the architect of your own future' to find work you love! Also:

- You are never too old to change
- Doing what you love will lead to fulfilment in your work and life
- Discover how balanced and how happy you are with your life
- Establish what needs to change and Why and start work on this now
- Do you want to be a 'wage slave' or break free and do what you love?

Congratulations! You are now ready to move to the next stage of the Cycle: **Establishing Your True Marketability**.

CHAPTER 3

Establishing Your True Marketability – Step 3

"When who you are aligns with what you do you will achieve extraordinary results."

Laura Berman Fortgang - Renowned Speaker, Author & Life Coach

What is your true marketability, you might be thinking? I get asked this question all the time. How does this differ from your marketability? The secret lies in Laura Berman Fortgang's fantastic quote. Establishing your *'true marketability'* is about **getting to know yourself, understanding who you are and what you have to offer the world.** This is so much more than establishing and marketing your transferable skills, which is what most people focus on. This step is where you really bring yourself to life by exploring and uncovering your 'complete personal package', which we will look at shortly. The insight you gain will move you from *'who am I'* to revelations about yourself that you may never have considered were possible. This is why Step 3 is at the heart of the Cycle and is an integral part of your career transition journey to help you move forward with renewed confidence, self-belief and motivation to change career.

As with Step 2, it is unlikely you will have done the type of in-depth analysis and 'soul searching' we will cover in Step 3. 'Digging deep' will make the process exciting and motivational with the exercises helping to unlock your potential, uncover hidden talents and open up new thinking about what opportunities might be possible for you in your career moving forward. I tell all my clients that Step 2 and Step 3 plus adopting the right mindset are what really make the difference to winning through career change. How good will it feel to know you can add powerful content to your CV, be more confident in interviews and sell yourself in a much more compelling and meaningful way? Equally, that you really do have the skills and potential to run your own business if you desire. Great, I'm sure.

In this Chapter we will explore:

- Understanding your true marketability so you can make this work for you

- Why it is important to be true to yourself and work from 'the inside out'
- Why you still have much work to do before sending out your CV
- Your complete package and what the 'bigger picture' entails
- Inspiring case studies of people who have used their true marketability to great effect
- Whether Personality Profiling may or may not help you
- Your Personal Brand and the importance of this to your career moving forward

Marketability

Why Is It So Important To Understand Your True Marketability?

First and foremost, you are probably like most people who greatly undersell and under value themselves and find it difficult to 'blow your own trumpet'. Unfortunately, the reality is that if you don't tell people how good you are, it is unlikely anyone else will. So, by understanding who you are and what you have to offer, this will help you:

- Get a much better handle on what might be possible for you to consider moving forward
- Determine whether you wish to be employed or self employed
- If you wish to be employed this key insight will help you rewrite your CV to be targeted, focused and sell you in the best light

- If you decide on self-employment, consider options for your business venture
- Determine whether a portfolio career is right for you as a result of your range of skills, talents, interests and passions
- Bring yourself to life so it will become easier to explain who you are and what you have to offer when meeting people informally or selling yourself in networking situations
- Achieve a big boost to your confidence and self-esteem by realising you have so much more to offer than you thought
- Move forward to the upward swing of the 'emotional roller coaster'
- To help you take control of interviews, if you learn how to use your newly gained knowledge effectively (see Julie and Sarah's case studies)

Working 'Inside Out' - Be True To Yourself And Life Will Be True To You

If you want to establish your '**true** marketability' you must be totally honest with yourself. Your thoughts must come from your heart. The majority of the exercises in this book will challenge you to think from 'your inside out'. This means you will be using your heart more than your head. The fundamental difference means that your responses are far more likely to represent the authentic you.

Working on 'an authentic you' will have the greatest impact on finding a job, career or work you love and leading a fulfilling lifestyle. Sometimes you might cloud the issue by taking shortcuts and trying to let your head control your heart. We will revisit this point when we look at Personality Profiling, one area where the head does take control.

Top tips for working through the exercises to be true to yourself

- Accept that getting to know your true self and what you have to offer, is at the heart of the Career Navigation Cycle hence don't be tempted to take short cuts
- Do not underestimate the amount of work, time, effort and mental energy you will need to spend on this crucial stage of the process
- Be patient and stick with the process as "you reap what you sow", as the saying goes
- You may find it easier and more rewarding to work in 'bite size chunks' so you can see gradual results from your efforts

Showcasing Yourself

CV = 'Curriculum Vitae' OR 'CircumVenting' The Process?

Consider this scenario:

You are looking to change career and at this stage you believe you need to look for another job so you immediately dust off your CV, consider updating it, adding relevant new information, then fire it out to as many companies, organisations, agencies and job boards as possible. Does this sound familiar? STOP and ask yourself this key question: Is this the best use of your time and course of action at this early stage? By taking this approach you will have joined the majority of job seekers blazing the same path. Do you want to be part of the sheep mindset or do you want to become the architect of your own future and take control of your life and career? The latter I'm sure sounds more appealing, doesn't it?

Interestingly, many career management consultancies and recruitment agencies will have you following exactly this route because it is arguably the 'easy' option, as in theory you can get cracking on your CV straight away. However, by taking this route and circumnavigating all the time consuming but crucial 'soul searching', you could easily end up 'out of the frying pan and into the fire' and I'm sure you don't want that, do you?

What Is Wrong With This Approach, I Hear You Say?

I know to my own cost and working with many clients over the last decade, that taking this approach at this early stage is often the biggest mistake that many career changers inadvertently make. Why? Because there is much work to be done before updating and rewriting your CV and blasting it out to 'the universe'. **Taking this approach is unlikely to get you on the interview 'YES' pile, unless you have first established and understood your true marketability and how this relates to your career change.** Without having done this work and taken this key step in the Career Navigation Cycle process, you are essentially 'putting the cart before the horse'.

In my experience, at this early stage of the Cycle process, your CV is most unlikely to be targeted, focused or sell you in the best light. Also, you really need to take a step back, follow the steps highlighted in Chapters 1 and 2 and then utilise all the nuggets in this Chapter, if you want to create maximum impact with your CV.

Your CV may even become virtually redundant, if you decide to pursue other options such as self-employment or a portfolio career. The unfortunate reality is that most people who have not worked their way through a career change before (and even some who have) will automatically feel obligated to be doing something positive towards finding your next job and therefore follow what seems to be the most obvious route to market. I can assure you the reality is very different.

Consider this scenario:

Imagine two CV's landing on an employer or recruiter's desk, - the first one is purely skills focused and the second one really brings the person to life in a very positive and powerful way so that their personality, work ethic, career objectives, achievements and energy leap off the page. Unless the skill level is the only prerequisite for the job, who are you going to invite to interview? The second one, I'm sure.

Developing an in depth self-awareness of who you are and what you have to offer is essential for effective self-marketing and developing your career. This provides focus and clarity to ensure that you are applying for the right jobs, your applications are targeted and you sell yourself in the best light on your CV and also in any networking or interview situations.

Please resist the temptation to shortcut the Career Navigation Cycle process as I can guarantee that 'more haste will become less speed'!

Whilst you might feel you are doing something positive (as the firing out of your CV to the universe may feel cathartic), this is what I call taking a classic 'scattergun' approach, where you fire lots of bullets but few, if any, will hit the target, as 'you can't hit a target you cannot see', can you?

How Circumnavigating The Process Can Adversely Impact The Interview Situation

If you should get called to an interview at this stage, you might be excited. However, unless this is as a result of some networking or from a previously known contact, this could be a result of more luck than judgement. As you won't have got to grips with who you are and what you have to offer and understand your true marketability yet, you are highly unlikely to sound compelling and give the best account of yourself at interview. Moreover, you will be like the majority of people (regardless of their level) who dramatically undersell themselves and lack confidence, which you will certainly need by the bucket load to sell yourself effectively into a new career. Equally importantly, you won't have worked through fully what sort of job or career is right for you. Therefore, even if you are offered the job, you risk the danger of yet another example of jumping 'out of the frying pan and into the fire', which you don't want, do you?

Another downside of applying for jobs before you have completed the key soul searching legwork is the negative emotional impact this will have on you. If you keep getting invited to interviews before you really understand your true marketability, you don't sell yourself effectively and are always unsuccessful, you actually start to dread, rather than desire, being invited to interviews.

I have seen this happen with many people (clients, friends and contacts) who have chosen to ignore my advice. You can easily go into a downward spiral, not wanting to apply for jobs for fear of rejection. This is when your motivation, confidence and self-esteem can be shot to pieces, as we covered in Chapter 1 and it can become a vicious circle. This is clearly not what you want is it, at this delicate stage of your career change process, just when you should be looking forward to starting on a positive upswing on your 'emotional roller coaster ride'?

Therefore resist the temptation to attend interviews until you are good and ready and motivated to get the right next job for you for all the right reasons. Once you have established your true marketability, worked through the Cycle and have achieved clarity, it is highly likely you will either be applying for jobs that are way beyond your current thinking, you will have found ways to circumnavigate the recruitment process or you may not even want to be employed anymore. Therefore continue to focus on working through the Cycle process and save yourself becoming unnecessarily distracted.

Your 'Package'

Skills Are Important - But They Are Only Part Of The Picture

Most career books and career consultancies highlight the importance of knowing your skills and especially transferable skills, when it comes to looking at a new job or career. This is absolutely right as of course these are always important. However, skills are only part of what you have to offer. Understanding the concept of *'true marketability'* as your 'complete package', 'the whole you' and what you have to offer, is a powerful process of self-discovery and one that will help you for the rest of your working life.

Skills are undeniably a vital ingredient for success in all job roles and for some the more specific or the more transferable the better. For some very specialist, technical and clinical jobs, having exactly the right skill set and proven ability to do the role could certainly be the determining factor. I'm sure you wouldn't want to be operated on by anything other than a top quality brain surgeon! However, *your true marketability* is your complete package of:

- Skills
- Attributes
- Attitude
- Strengths
- Achievements
- Knowledge
- Connections
- Interests
- Passions
- Values
- Personal Brand

Skills will always be important and the more transferable the better. However, as I have said, they do not provide the full picture. It is a fact that most skills can be learnt or developed and you can always plug skills gaps by going on courses or finding a mentor, as we will look at later on in the book. Conversely, when looking at attributes and attitude it is harder to change your personality, nature and outlook on life. The old adage that 'a leopard can never change its spots' is true to an extent. However, you **can change** but only by working really hard to develop and grow personally to have a positive impact on who you are and how you approach life. It is also a fact that 'you never get a second chance to create a first impression'. Therefore if what you see is what you get, then enthusiastic, positive people, radiating energy, become infectious, so why would you not want to be one too? These points all illustrate that your true marketability is so much more than your skills.

The Bigger Picture

Marketable means that you are sought after and in demand. Your true marketability is the value you offer an employer or the marketplace in terms of your complete package. You can now see by **Establishing Your True Marketability** that **this is an infinitely more powerful proposition than just focusing on your skills.** Enthusiasm, determination, drive, energy, passion, willingness to learn and a positive 'can do' attitude can leapfrog you over the competition, even when they have more experience and 'better skills'. *Why?* Because such attributes and attitude can add real value to most jobs and organisations, whether this is for employed roles or to win work or contracts if you are self-employed.

So what do you have 'for sale' that you can offer to an employer or to your clients if you decide to set up your own business? If this sounds like a difficult question, don't worry, as we will go through a number of exercises to help you flesh out this key information. You can start to work on identifying your unique selling points or propositions (USPs). For USPs think *what makes you different or better* than your competition? Consider how difficult it would be for you to establish this without first having dug really deep, as we will do with some of the forthcoming exercises? I cannot stress this strongly enough, regardless of the level you are working at or aspiring to, the majority of people greatly undersell themselves. In today's fiercely competitive job market, by establishing and really accentuating your true marketability, you will stand out from the crowd. This also becomes of great importance when we look at your personal brand, at the end of this Chapter.

The following case study is an excellent example of getting to grips with your true marketability and being able to see the 'bigger picture', past your previous jobs, to get you ahead of the competition.

Julie's Story

Julie, married to a Brit, is a delightful French woman who was determined to settle down in the UK and carve out a career for herself and eventually start a family. Her career had previously been in a number of support roles but she had never found her true passion. Following her last role, in which she was frustrated and unsettled, she decided to travel round Europe with her new husband. What started as an adventure and escape from their dull working routine for a few months, turned into a couple of years travelling and working their way around Europe. Eventually, they felt it was time to return, get back to reality, 'proper jobs' and get themselves on the property ladder.

When I asked Julie 'what was holding her back', she told me employers were not taking her seriously because they expected her to go off travelling again, so were not prepared to take the risk in recruiting her. In addition, she felt she was always falling short of the required skills highlighted on job descriptions, so either did not apply for some jobs or rarely got an interview. If she did get an interview, it became apparent to me that she was talking herself out of the job by her lack of belief in herself and what she had to offer. She also felt lacking in not having certain qualifications that were 'required' in some of the jobs for which she applied.

The turning point was getting Julie to open up and focus on some of the amazing experiences from her travels. Focusing on her achievements, the wide range of skills she had used, some of the weird and wonderful jobs she had done while travelling and above all else, her passion to work with disadvantaged people with learning difficulties and make a difference to their lives helped Julie see a new future. This was to become a new and very different Julie!

I worked intently with Julie and impressed on her that passion, desire, hunger, enthusiasm, positive attitude, willingness to learn and many similar attributes and attitudes could win the day against more experienced competition 'with the required piece of paper'. Julie was initially unconvinced and could not see past having the required qualifications. I shared with her similar examples of other clients I had worked with over the years who proved my point beyond all shadow of doubt. She realised she had classic limiting beliefs around her true marketability. What she had believed up to now was her perception rather than reality. This was her first breakthrough!

Julie then landed an interview for her 'dream job' at a local college, supporting young people with learning difficulties. However, she was still convinced she would not get the job and was only there to 'make up the numbers'. The fact that she had achieved an interview already proved my point that they considered her a strong candidate. Why would they bother otherwise?

Key point - You must have the core belief, that if you get invited to an interview, you will have a fighting chance of getting the job. This is an important reframe, so you can show confidence, self-belief and be positive in your ability to get the job.

So, first part of the job done but Julie now had to nail the interview. It is not my intention to cover interview skills in great detail in this book, as the focus is very different.

Although I do much coaching and training around interview skills, there are plenty of other excellent books and resources readily available. However, I worked with Julie on answering key questions; especially the dreaded 'tell me about yourself', which is many people's nightmare question and maybe yours too?

Julie tended to ramble on about travelling Europe with her husband for the past few years. Instead, I got her to focus on what she had learnt from the experience, some of the skills she had developed along the way, how the experience had changed her thinking about life, how adaptable and flexible she had learnt to become and above all else, how she was now passionate about giving back and making a difference to the lives of less fortunate young people. What we did was to work really hard on her true marketability; i.e., the things that made her who she is and what she really had to offer in relation to the job. The result... Julie got the job! Not only did she get the job, she did so being the only person to make the shortlist who was not formally 'qualified'. This feedback was volunteered by the line manager who stated in no uncertain terms that, despite not having the desired (not required) qualification, Julie blew the interview panel away with her amazing passion and enthusiasm, but most importantly her willingness to learn and genuine desire to make a difference.

What a great result and amazing transformation! This inspiring case study encapsulates so much of what I have covered in the first two Chapters in terms of the power of your thinking and mindset, which are crucial factors to making a successful career change.

Unlock Your True Potential!

"Your attitude, not your aptitude, will determine your altitude"

Zig Ziglar - Author and Motivational Speaker

I love this wonderful quote from the enigmatic Zig Ziglar, an inspirational personal development guru, who unfortunately passed away a few years ago. I believe his quote exemplifies what can be achieved if you really understand your true marketability because then you can sell yourself with maximum effectiveness, impact and confidence. You are learning some important lessons from these inspiring case studies so let's now build on this and take a look at some great ways to flesh out your true marketability and really unlock **your** potential.

How? Where Do I Start?

The starting point is to identify your natural talents and also hidden talents. This is often a revelation as you discover things about your skills, attributes and attitude that you may never have considered. The process of positive self-discovery should also give you a real confidence boost! To help you achieve greater clarity of who you are and what you have to offer, the Proudest Achievements and Self-Awareness Matrix are powerful exercises to help you unlock your potential and passions you may not have considered.

✎ *Exercise - Your Proudest Achievements*

Do you ever think back to when you were 'invincible' or when you achieved something significant or remarkable in your life? In my case, it was when I was 23 and decided to up sticks and travel to Australia. The whole planning process, my amazing adventures, challenges and experiences undoubtedly helped to change my life and shape who I am today. Regardless of what stage you are at in your life, I would like you to reflect and identify some of your proudest achievements. This is a very powerful exercise if you apply yourself by being totally committed to the task, as you need to be with the entire Career Navigation Cycle process. So here we go:

Step 1

Clear your mind and consider a couple of your favourite achievements. These should be things that you are very proud of and make you feel good thinking about them. They should be personal to you so don't worry about whether other people think these are your 'best' achievements as it is important to choose what feels right for you.

Note – only one achievement should be work related and one (or more) totally non work related. *Why?* - Because it is usually the achievements outside the workplace that reveal the skills, attributes, attitudes, knowledge, learning and so on that can help to uncover your hidden talents, unlock your potential and open up new thinking and opportunities!

Step 2

Write up each achievement as a short story in whatever way works best for you, e.g. using your computer or on a sheet of paper using the following process:

- What you set out to do and WHY?
- The challenge - what was in your way?
- Step by step - what was your approach?
- The result - what was the outcome of your efforts?
- The meaning - how did it make you feel?

Step 3

When you have completed each story, read through and list as many skills and attributes as possible that you feel you demonstrated in the process of your achievement. You will more than likely find this difficult (it is!) but persevere, as you will gain much benefit from the output.

Step 4

To gain another perspective and add to your list of skills and attributes, share your stories with people you know, trust and value their opinions and ask them to list skills, attributes, attitudes and even knowledge. You might just be surprised what they come up with!

Step 5

Now consider what you have learnt from this exercise. What is the output telling you? Also, how do you feel having fleshed out such useful and positive information about yourself? If you are like the vast majority of people who do this exercise, you will come to realise it is always much harder for us to see the good in ourselves. It is always easier to see others' good qualities. Also, we often overlook the obvious as we 'can't see the wood for the trees!'

✎ *Exercise - The Self-Awareness Matrix*

Let's now continue building the picture with another great exercise that will really challenge your thinking and help to unlock your potential and passions. This exercise may look innocuous but it helped to transform my thinking and has done the same thing for many of my clients. *Why?* For a couple of simple but key reasons:

1. Just because you are good at something doesn't mean to say you enjoy it the most

2. You may have never considered your passions and interests could be potential income opportunities!

Note: This is not an easy exercise. If you are struggling with this, or any other of the exercises, especially in this key Step and Chapter, you will find some useful video and audio clips of myself and other successful clients explaining them on my inspirational and innovative Online Career Change Programme:

http://www.steveprestonthecareercatalyst.com/online-career-change-programme/

Attracts/Interests/ Inspires (Passions)	***Best at***
Experience package (skills, knowledge, attributes/attitude)	***Enjoy most***

Unlocking your Potential and Passions: the Self-Awareness Matrix will help you uncover:

- What attracts, interests and inspires you
- What you most enjoy doing

- What you are best at
- Any additional knowledge, skills or attributes
- Recurring themes from your career and life thus far
- What you enjoy and want to continue doing
- What you enjoy and maybe don't want to continue doing
- A whole raft of possibilities to consider and review!

Step 1

You can set this matrix up on a Word document or similar on your computer or use a minimum A4 size sheet of paper, as you will need plenty of space to write in each quadrant.

Step 2

Completely open your mind and be prepared to stretch your thinking. You now have a blank canvas to create something new and exciting! **Think about all aspects of life not just work.**

Step 3

Start writing in the quadrant you relate to the most or you find easiest and use words or statements that reflect how you feel, e.g. **Enjoy The Most** might be helping people

Step 4

The Experience Package quadrant is the only one that is 'absolute', i.e. this is related to skills and attributes from your career and life. You can transpose the skills and attributes you have fleshed out from the Proudest Achievements exercise plus any others that now spring to mind. Also, specific knowledge you have that is clearly part of who you are.

Step 5

Keep adding words and statements in each quadrant until you run out of steam. **If you feel a word or statement fits in more than one quadrant add it to each one it applies to.** This is very important as it is sending you a powerful message you should not ignore.

Step 6

Keep challenging yourself and drill down to another level e.g. if you had 'helping others', what is it about helping others you enjoy the most or are best at? This way you will get even more specific information you can then work with.

Step 7

Look for the common themes that appear in multiple quadrants, especially 3 or all 4. These are really important as you are getting powerful messages that you ignore at your peril!

Step 8

As with the Proudest Achievements exercise, ask trusted, valued friends and contacts to tell you '*what you are best at*'. Make the point that this is not just about work but anything they feel relevant about you as a person in life in general. Add their comments to your matrix. If you find this exercise too difficult to complete on your own, I suggest you work with a Coach or someone you can open up to who will ask you challenging questions around your story. It is important you keep adding to the matrix as you get new inspiration and 'light bulb moments'. This is a work in progress as you continue the book and work your way round the Cycle.

What have you got?

You should now have a whole raft of information about yourself which you can start to explore in more depth. What are the common themes in multiple quadrants? What are these telling you about yourself and possibilities for future jobs or work? Compare the output against your proudest achievements exercise and consider whether a picture is starting to emerge? Are there any surprises? If so what are they? Also, can you see themes emerging around skills and attributes which always appear when you achieve anything worthwhile or when you do work you love? This leads nicely into the next section.

The Importance Of Understanding Your Motivated Abilities

Your Motivated Abilities are your natural gifts or talents, things you gravitate towards without even thinking, e.g. favourite skills and attributes. Other ways of looking at your motivated abilities are: Your inner motivation, what makes you tick and depending on your outlook, some people also use terms such as, 'your natural DNA' and 'your unique calling'. These are the skills, attributes and recurring strengths that are always at the heart of any achievements in your life. By understanding these motivated abilities you can make sure they feature in your everyday work in the future. This way you can create a fulfilling life and maximise your true potential. I'm sure this sounds appealing, doesn't it?

✎ *Exercise - Motivated Abilities*

The good news is you can now start to uncover your motivated abilities using the output from the previous two exercises. Now to dig even deeper with this simple but effective exercise!

1. Look at your list of skills and attributes and consider which of these you can now see are the ones you naturally gravitate towards and feature when you are

at your happiest. Also, those which, on reflection, you realise always feature when you have achieved anything worthwhile in your life.

2. Highlight these skills and attributes so you can start to focus your energy on them. Imagine how you can use them in a different environment, career or type of work.

3. Also now consider other skills and attributes you naturally use, which if they did not feature in a future job or career, would seem like you were missing a key part of you.

You now have some immensely powerful information about yourself that is a key part of your true marketability and which can help to shape your future!

Mo's Story

We all have a tendency to 'undersell' ourselves, but this is the greatest!

I will now share with you a most extreme example of someone who was blissfully unaware of their true marketability. This is an inspiring story of a client who had some amazing hidden talents and motivated abilities and how by uncovering these, his thinking changed and then he changed his life. Please read carefully, as you, like Mo, could take the learning from this story to change your life. That would be an amazing feeling, wouldn't it?

A number of years ago I was running a group career change workshop for professionals. I had just introduced the concept of the 'Self-Awareness Matrix' to the group. They all understood what needed to be done except one person who challenged me by saying, 'I cannot think of anything outside of work and I know there is no work to be had in my field in the UK as it is so specialist, so what else can I do to make this exercise work for me?'

I was aware that Mo had come over to the UK from the US post 9/11, when he did not have the right papers. Mo did work in a very specialist field of fire protection and there was only one company in the UK who did this type of work and they had no jobs available at the time. He had not found work of any sort and was really struggling to keep focused and motivated, as could not see past his previous job title. I questioned him on what else he was attracted to, what he did outside of work, what hobbies he had and so on. The answer that came back was always 'nothing' or 'none'. Undeterred and not to be beaten, I then asked him if he did any work in the community or voluntary work. What you are about to read will hopefully, like me and all of group that day, blow your mind!

Mo shared with the group that he 'was involved with the refurbishment of his local mosque'. I asked him what sort of activities this involved. Although this was a number of years ago, it is still fresh in my mind and went something along these lines:

He had to:

1. Organise for planning permission with the local authority
2. Help with drawing up the refurbishment plans
3. Find a suitable building company to carry out the work
4. Muster up a large team of dozens of volunteers
5. Create a budget for the refurbishment
6. Manage and monitor the budget
7. Keep track of the work being done, etc. etc.!

Then a couple of fantastic throwaway comments: "And we managed to do everything on time and within budget" to which the group pointed out this never happens in 'the real world'! Then another real showstopper: "I forgot I also organised the relaunch party in the park opposite. I contacted the Mayor, local press and media and organised a massive firework display. The Mayor opened the ceremony and thousands of people turned up including the local BBC news team who interviewed me for London News. It was a great success!" Watching everyone's body language in the room was unbelievable as most people were sitting totally spellbound with their mouths wide open like goldfish. I asked Mo what his story was telling us. One of the group chipped in and asked if he had considered taking up project management? Remarkably there was still confusion on his face and he replied totally seriously 'I wouldn't know where to start"! By this time the room was full of laughter from total disbelief at his response before one of the group piped up saying "you have just given us the most amazing example of successful project management, so what are you talking about!"

Only then did he register what was happening and he had the most amazing light bulb moment.

Mo shared that he had secretly thought about setting up a business with his wife, an interior designer and "What if I went out finding and managing projects and she did the feminine soft interior touches?" To say this was a career defining moment was the understatement of the century! It also proved, yet again, that most people have little idea of their true talents and capabilities and can only think of themselves in relation to the jobs they have done in their careers. This is another key reason why people undersell themselves so dramatically - they really don't understand what they do have to offer. Yet here was the most extreme example of someone blessed with some fantastic skills, attributes and an undeniable natural talent or motivated ability for managing projects. This was reconfirmed when Mo recalled other, much smaller projects, outside the workplace he had successfully managed in the past!

What can you learn from Mo?

One minute he was incapable of considering doing anything other than the job he had trained for his entire career and next minute he was visualising a new career, the joy of setting up a business with his wife and making a success of it! Truly amazing and I felt privileged to have facilitated and witnessed such an immediate transformation.

I have come across many similar examples where people are totally oblivious to skills and talents and attributes they possess. Mo's story proves emphatically, once you take the blinkers off and come to terms with your true marketability and motivated abilities the only thing that can stop you achieving a similar success is guess what? Yes... you!

In terms of the Career Navigation Cycle, Mo in one fell swoop had:

- Let go and was looking forward (Step 1)
- Understood what was important to him in his career and life and WHY (Step 2)
- Uncovered many of his hidden talents, passions and his true marketability (Step 3)
- Started to think about exploring new opportunities (Step 4)

This just shows how powerful the insights gained from his amazing achievement were, in proving to him that he did have lots of great skills and attributes. Therefore, if Mo could deliver such a massive project on time and to budget then anything was possible. This was invaluable reassurance, which is something we all need to motivate us and spur us on. In a flash Mo had moved 3 steps round the Cycle!

I'm sure you too have also had achievements in your life that you have just brushed over and taken for granted, rather than looking more closely to see how remarkable they really were?

By taking the learning from such examples, you will challenge and change your thinking about what you have to offer the world and what work you can now consider. With this in mind, get cracking to see what inspiration and exciting light bulb moments you uncover!

Personal Profiling

How About Personality Or Psychometric Profiling?

Now you have uncovered your many skills, attributes and motivated abilities, is there an argument for you to also do some personality or psychometric profiling? If so, what is it and how might it help you? There are a multitude of personality profiling tools available these days, which can measure your behaviours, temperament, communication style, strengths, how you work in a team, leadership style and ability and many variations on these themes. It is easy to get lost in the range of options. Some can even be done free online. However, these are usually cut down versions of the full paid for profiles and often you will need to pay for the main report or follow up coaching.

Coaches, like me, will need to be trained and accredited before they can give professional feedback on such tools. While many reports are fairly self-explanatory, most of the real 'nuggets' are hidden in the information that is not obvious, so while some freebies are OK, they will only provide a part of the picture. There are also some career profiling tools, which are aimed at narrowing down potential options for future careers. My experience of these is that they can often confuse rather than clarify and you can sometimes end up with an A-Z list of career options, like something out of a Monty Python sketch! Remember there is no 'holy grail' or quick fix.

Personally, I am accredited for DISC, which I like because it is very transparent, it has always proven to be very accurate and the reports are very well constructed and user friendly.

How do these tools measure up against some of the exercises in this book?

Unlike the exercises you have completed in this book, which you can do in your own time and at your own pace, being honest and from your heart, it is important to understand that personality and psychometric profiling requires you to answer multiple questions within an allotted time, e.g. anything from 10 minutes to 45 minutes depending on the complexity and number of questions. The nature of these profiles means you need to answer with your immediate gut reaction. Although it is good to trust your gut instincts, as we have covered previously, when you are bombarded with a raft of similar questions with multiple choice possibilities for answers, e.g. strongly agree, disagree, etc., you can feel pressured to come up with an answer just to move onto the next question, so you tend to answer from your head rather than your heart.

Your mindset will also play a big part, so the results are likely to be very contextual, depending on what stage of the 'emotional roller coaster' you are at. I tend to use such profiling sparingly, mainly when the client has never had experience of such analysis, so that these will be new revelations. Also, where the client may have done profiling years ago, they may be keen to see what has changed and work through why this is so, which can be most beneficial.

For managers, leaders, top professionals and executives, understanding your emotional intelligence (EQ) and how best to use this can be a great benefit. Many organisations are coming to the realisation that having high EQ is of greater benefit as a leader than high IQ. You only have to look at Sir Richard Branson and Lord Alan Sugar as two wonderful examples. Emotional Intelligence is a big subject in its own right but one I would recommend you learn more about if you want to know how to get the best out of your 'emotional capacity' to influence and impact on others. This is a key part of understanding your personal brand, which we will be exploring next.

Although most profiling tends to be a fairly good assessment of the person, because of some of the concerns mentioned, some people berate such tools, as they don't believe them to be an accurate reflection of themselves. The reality might be that it is an accurate snapshot of you in that moment.

I have found when clients have done such profiling during restructuring or as part of a redeployment selection process, the results are often skewed. You might be tempted to answer how you believe you want to be perceived by your employer rather than what you believe yourself. This rather defeats the object and you are ultimately going to get found out.

Also, I would caution against thinking that by doing some personality profiling you will shortcut the Cycle process. The output from any profiling, although helpful, is only a small part of who you are and what you have to offer, so a fraction of your true marketability. Remember follow and believe in the Six Step process. There are no shortcuts and more haste = less speed!

Brand 'YOU'

We have looked at many aspects of your true marketability, all of which are crucial in helping you understand more about yourself and what you have to offer to help you navigate your way to a brighter future. In the final piece of your true marketability jigsaw, we will explore the importance of your Personal Brand and how to make this work for you.

I have said consistently throughout this book, that the majority of people greatly undersell and under value themselves. By developing your personal brand, you have an opportunity to be much clearer about the authentic you and what you have to offer the world. Developing your personal brand therefore should be a key part of any self -marketing strategy, regardless of whether you decide to look for a different type of job, become self-employed or develop a portfolio career.

Personal Brand – Stand Out From The Crowd

Personal branding is about what makes you unique or 'remarkable'. It relates to how people see you, what you project to others and their perception of you. The key to building your brand is therefore to know yourself and aim to be the best possible you!

Your personal brand identity is about:

- Your image

- How you look
- Your behaviours
- How you communicate
- Your reputation
- How you make others feel
- The impact you make

We have already covered the fact it is so much easier to see things in other people than it is in ourselves. This makes it all the more important to get the right feedback on how people really do perceive you from a number of perspectives. Understanding, developing and managing your personal brand builds on the work you have already been doing in this Chapter. Your future career depends on your ability to effectively communicate you, your thoughts and ideas in a confident, clear and compelling way. Imagine the difference this will make for you at interviews, when networking or in client meetings? Much more confident, I'm sure.

The best way to market and position yourself is by developing your personal brand, as the better you are at getting your personal brand to work for you the less you need to sell yourself. Let's face it, selling ourselves is what most of us hate doing, isn't it? That said, having a branded message, which is authentic about who you are and what makes you distinctive, will be an important ingredient to your success. However, at this stage of the Cycle, you might not be ready to launch your branded message out to the universe, might you? This is more than likely another work in progress, isn't it? If so, why not play with such messages and test them out on family, friends and close contacts first to gauge their reaction. You can fine tune your message over time, as you will be in a much better position to have developed an authentic message you feel comfortable and confident with by the time you complete this book.

To define your personal brand identity you have to discover who you are and what differentiates you. You have already covered much of this work in previous exercises in this Chapter and Chapter 2. Your personal brand identity is an amalgamation of your assets (skills, attributes, natural talents and life experiences), your values (the things that matter to you) as well as your passions and your image (what you project to others). Importantly, it is also how you look, behave, sound and how you make others feel. It's what you measure everything you do against, for example:

- How you meet and greet people
- The way you react or respond to others
- How you follow up
- How you listen
- Your empathy with others
- How you manage colleagues
- The questions you ask
- How you come across in presentations
- How you run meetings
- The way you dress
- How you engage others
- Your outlook on life
- Your overall persona

Your brand identity is what makes you stand out from the crowd, as an individual. With modern technology, your brand identity is also about your 'communication tools', e.g. your Smartphone, iPad, tablet or laptop. Are you an Apple or Android person and why? Also your networks, how you develop and manage these is of utmost and increasing importance. We will look at how you manage your online reputation through social media and blogs in Chapter 4. In summary, the definition I like best is *"your personal brand identity is what people say about you when you're not in the room".* This says it all, don't you think?

Ask Others You Know, Trust & Value

Personal Brand Development, to bring you to life in a compelling way, is a relatively new concept in the UK. It has attained a much higher profile in the US to date, but things are now changing, as the global marketplace becomes ever more competitive. In order to really explore your personal brand, you also need to know yourself from the feedback from others. For some of the questions related to the exercises in this section, it will pay you to ask the same people you have asked previously for feedback, especially the Self-Awareness Matrix and Proudest Achievement exercises. This way you can look for consistency from trusted and valued contacts.

If you are looking to progress your career you tend to be more aware of the fact that you need to do something positive about managing your image and reputation. If you are changing career completely, then the same is also true. *Why?* Because you could be known for having a career, in, let's say, the IT industry and are seen as a particular type of person. If you now decide to change to a completely different career or start your own business, this suddenly puts you in a very different light. You will almost certainly need to project yourself in a different way to create maximum impact. This is why so many people hold back from making such a change, as the thought of reinventing yourself and your brand can be quite scary, as we saw with Jane in Chapter 1. However, you don't want to be like this do you? I thought not! Therefore, you will need to work through these exercises and gradually develop your new personal brand identity over time, as you find your new life path.

✎ *Exercise - Creating Your Personal Brand Using The 5 Ps*

Defining your personal brand

As a starter to the main exercise, write down key words or statements which you believe reflect who you are and what you have to offer, that you believe are the authentic you.

Ask yourself does your personal brand have the right impact to aid your success, your new career choice (if you have one) or does it undersell you?

This is a big area and one where it really pays to work with a personal branding and impact coach. Debbie Smith, who works with executives and professionals, is a specialist in this field and also a key associate in my company team.

Personal Branding is a big subject, so for this book, we will focus on **Purpose, Passions, Personal Presence, Perception and Product.**

Defining your vision and purpose

To build your brand you must have a clear picture of who you are, where you're going and how you're going to get there. As you might have gathered this is not an easy task but stick with it, as you will reap the rewards.

You may not have a clear picture of your vision yet, but if you do, write it down somewhere you can see it. You can then constantly and regularly revisit it to motivate yourself to achieve the goal.

(i) Your Purpose

A great exercise to help you to establish this is to imagine yourself at your own funeral. I know this might sound morbid but you will see why this can be helpful when you've done it. Imagine you can hear what people are saying about you, what you've accomplished, how you touched their lives, your legacy, how you made a difference to them. Their comments suggest your purpose. What are they saying about you? Write down what you're hearing. This can be very powerful to help you move forward. You may have never thought this way about your purpose before.

(ii) Your Passions

Your passions are the activities that most energise you. In addition to being perceived as a high performer, your passions will also make you memorable. Using the work you have done from 'Your Proudest Achievements' and the Self-Awareness Matrix exercise, list 10 things which will make your life and work ideal. Then list your top 5. Put them in priority order of most passionate as number 1. Describe *'what does that look like?'* Describe each one in as much detail as you can. This will help you to bring your passions to life.

(iii) Personal Presence

"Like it or not people will always be judged on their appearance as well as their abilities and in the current climate some bosses will be reassessing their workforce, so it's prudent to look the part as well as acting it".

Professor Khalid Aziz, Business Journalist & Author

Managing your appearance to direct attention to where you want it, from potential employers, clients and people in your own circles is essential in determining the success of your brand. When your image is polished and refined, your personal presence conveys a grounded and trustworthy person... someone with whom people want to interact with and do business. When your image is out of balance, your personal presence is compromised and may send unintended signals to the very people you want to positively influence. How you dress and your general presence says much about your person and needs to be consistent with the type of work and people with whom you mix.

(iv) Perception

What are others' perceptions of you as a person? How you look, behave, work, your image, reputation, and so on? **What do people say about you when you are not in the room?** Find out and write this down so you can work on this constantly as you move your career forward, regardless of what you end up doing.

(v) Your Product

To sell and market yourself successfully it really helps to think of yourself as a product. You need to create a desirable 'package' for your product that will make you remarkable!

How you package yourself, your skills, attributes, knowledge and talents will ultimately determine the effectiveness of your 'campaign', whether in or out of work.

- What are your special skills and talents?
- What are you selling to potential employers or clients if you plan to set up your own business? If you know, write it down and focus on it. If not, you can return to this later, once you have completed Steps 4 and 5 of the Cycle.
- **What makes you remarkable, different or better** than other people you are competing against? If you know, write it down and focus on it. If not, again you can return to this later, once you have completed Steps 4 and 5 of the Cycle.

- Is your product (i.e. you) appropriately priced?
- Do you understand your true worth or are you underselling or overselling yourself?
- Do you need to make improvements (e.g. acquire more skills) to command the salary or package you are aspiring to?

So many questions and not enough answers?

You may not know the answers to some of these questions at this stage of the process. Don't worry as it will pay you to revisit this section regularly, once you start to see a new picture emerging, or when you have completed the book and the six steps of the Cycle. The more work you do around your personal brand and creating an authentic you the more people will talk about you in glowing, positive terms when you are out of the room or online, and the greater your chances of achieving success in life. To put this into perspective, the following case study is a brilliant example. It encapsulates many of the key points from this Chapter around **Establishing Your True Marketability** (including your personal brand) and how to use the learning from this 'work in progress' to successfully reinvent you, redesign your career and do work you love.

Jes's Story - Turning your true marketability into opportunities

A successful General Manager, Jes reached a pinnacle in his career by helping his company achieve a prized nationally acclaimed customer service award. Instead of championing his efforts, his 'reward' was to be treated very shoddily by his employer which resulted in his position becoming untenable and taking them to an Employment Tribunal. Jes was 'lost 'and in a bad place after a spate of bad luck followed. He decided to take positive action and sought refuge on one of my early Breakthrough Career Change & Transition Masterclasses.

The 'Proudest Achievement' exercise was to become an amazing catalyst for him. Jes holds the record for having six full pages of flip chart paper plastered around the wall with his skills and attributes. This was truly amazing! His immediate reaction was "Is that me?" Of course it was. I merely facilitated the process and helped Jes get all the information out on paper. You could see the immediate change in his demeanour and the light bulb came on as he was wowed by the amazing revelations. Yes, he could change and his possibilities were endless!

What followed is interesting because Jes was fighting against the evidence which suggested he had a great skill set to become a Consultant and maybe set up his own consultancy business. At the time, he felt that was a bridge too far and he couldn't see it at all. This was a limiting belief. Self-employment was probably too scary when he had so many other key challenges in his life, not least financial.

One of his key passions, which emerged from the Masterclass, was writing. However he never previously pursued this interest. However, having come away from the day with renewed confidence, energy, motivation and focus, Jes very quickly secured some freelance work, writing reviews for luxury hotels around the world. This was a fantastic way of bringing together his travel background and his passion for writing. It also belied his thinking that he couldn't be self-employed and what a tough first 'gig'! He did this for a number of months before being headhunted as Sales and Marketing Director for a UK hotel chain. Jes saw this as a natural career change for him and a 'safer' option, being in a full-time employed role.

Interestingly, it took that experience for Jes to finally come to the realisation that he wanted to be the architect of his own future, take control of his destiny and should be running his own business. A couple of years after attending the Masterclass, that's exactly what he did. Jes set up his own leisure marketing company and is now doing very nicely. He is enjoying life once more, following his passions, constantly travelling the world with his business, developing new skills and a strong personal brand. He has also teamed up with a good contact, using their complimentary skills and a great network of contacts to mutual benefit and never looked back!

What does Jes's case study prove?

For some people, although all the evidence suggests self-employment and setting up a business of your own is a logical career change, as in Jes's case, the timing may not be right for you. However, once the seed has been planted, this is bound to be your final destination. Park it for now but keep it in your sights maybe as a medium or longer term goal while you explore other opportunities.

Following the steps of Career Navigation Cycle can have a profound impact. The process of self-discovery can prove a massive boost to your self-confidence and self-esteem. This is especially so when you unlock your potential to establish your true marketability. You then realise that you have far more to offer the world than you think. This will empower you, enable you to promote yourself in the best possible light and will help you to start building your personal brand whether you wish to be employed or self-employed.

How are you feeling about yourself now and what you have to offer the world?

With your new found insight, like Jes, Julie and Mo, you too can reinvent yourself

PIT STOP

WINNING STEER

Mark's Story (continued)

3

Step 3 – Establishing Your True Marketability

A physical guy, now really taking his exercise seriously.

Mark had worked hard to take stock and re-evaluate at Step 2, but it was his mindset that was holding him back. He could not see past his present job, which is very common. He had little or no understanding of who he was and what he had to offer an employer, which impacted on his confidence to sell himself.

Mark had come a long way and had much to be proud of, however, this time he had to dig deep to establish his true marketability and unlock his potential. Thankfully it was the self-awareness exercises given in this Chapter that enabled Mark to flesh out some great skills and personal attributes that in turn allowed him to see himself in quite a different light.

It's all well and good to identify skills and attributes that you didn't realise you had and this sudden insight is regularly experienced by people I am coaching. However, once Mark was equipped with this valuable information ...what was he going to do with it that would produce results?...

...to be continued

PIT STOP WINNING STEER

- The focus on the challenging exercises revealed that Mark was indeed very marketable with some great transferable skills, positive attributes and attitude

- Although Mark now had a greater understanding of himself, his potential and what to offer a new employer – the battle really was for him to believe this!
- Now facing the dilemma of making yet another career change how could he maximise his newly found self-awareness to help him transition from a physically demanding job he no longer desired?

Summary

- Your true marketability is your 'complete package', so much more than your skills
- Unlock your potential to uncover who you are and what you have to offer the world
- Establishing and understanding your true marketability is key to winning through career change and a successful career transition and can be a massive personal boost
- Avoid the 'scattergun' - resist the temptation to shortcut the Cycle process and fire out your CV before you have done the real hard graft and 'soul searching'
- More haste = less speed
- Skills are important but even more so are your attributes and "*Your attitude, not your aptitude, will determine your altitude*"
- Your motivated abilities are your natural talents. They will always appear as recurring themes of successes and achievements. Get to know and love them and embrace them to lead a fulfilling life
- Don't be held back by your limiting beliefs about who you are and what you have to offer

- If the evidence is staring you in the face, don't ignore it but work with it to determine your short, medium and longer term goals
- Passion, desire, enthusiasm, positive mindset and all these great attributes can win the day against more experienced and 'skilled' competition
- Personality profiling is helpful and part of your marketability but not the answer to everything
- Work from the inside out - use your heart first then your head and be true to yourself
- Ask for honest opinions from others you know, trust and value to help answer key questions in order to establish your true marketability and personal brand
- Your personal brand is important - while you are still working never stop developing your brand, as it is what sells you

Congratulations, you have come to the half way stage of the Career Navigation Cycle! You now have lots of fantastic information about yourself to really challenge your thinking. You are now ready to move to Step 4 of the Career Navigation Cycle – **Exploring Opportunities**. Before you do this, let's look at what we have covered on the journey so far:

- Step 1 - you will have learnt how to 'let go' and move forward
- Step 2 - you will now have a much better understanding of what is important to you in your career and life and WHY this is important to you
- Step 3 - you have uncovered who you are and what you have to offer the world!

Before you move on to Chapter 4, I suggest you might want to pause for breath and review the good work you have done to date. Reflection and review is a key part of the career change and transition process.

Often you will start to see things in a different light when looking a second time. However, it is your CHOICE, as it is important to work at your own pace and build momentum in the way that works best for you.

Additional Inspiration

If you are finding the going tough at this point or you want some more inspiration to keep you or get you back on track, you will definitely benefit from investing in my innovative and inspirational *'Navigate Your Way To A Brighter Future – 6 steps to transform your career & life'*Online Career Change and Transition programme. Clients have said it is *'Not just inspirational but transformational and works brilliantly well in tandem with this book to bring it to life for you'*. Check it out via this link:

http://www.steveprestonthecareercatalyst.com/online-career-change-programme/

CHAPTER 4

Exploring Opportunities – Step 4

"You have to go into the dark to find the gold"

Now you have reached the half way stage of the Cycle, this is where you need to harness all the information and wonderful nuggets you have learnt about yourself from Steps 1 to 3 of the process, to combine this with focus on the 'outer self' career development part of the Cycle. It's important that you up your game, as you will be constantly challenging yourself to bring the pieces of the jigsaw together to help you ultimately decide what to do next. This is likely to involve some difficult decisions, openly facing more of your fears and possibly breaking the pattern of conditioning which might have been ingrained from many years of work, parental thinking and influences from your friends and peers.

For many people this part of the process can become daunting because you've never had to dig this deep before. Although you have lots of powerful information to work with and may have come up with some great ideas, it is natural to experience self-doubts around your ability to make change happen in the way that's right for you. If so, don't worry as this Chapter will guide you through what works and what doesn't. You will learn key techniques to help you explore and open up new opportunities, as it is unlikely you will want to be in the same position in six months' time, will you?

In this Chapter we will explore:

- How you can put your ideas into place
- How to find the right opportunities for you
- Changing career within your organisation
- How to sell your 'new' self in the best way
- How to tap into the hidden job market
- The importance of social media
- Developing and optimizing your online and offline networks

- How to overcome your fears
- Some key mistakes to avoid
- Some key strategies to keep you focused and on track
- Turning talents and passions into profits!

Slotting Together The Pieces Of The Puzzle

Moving Through The Darkness And Towards The Light

You can now see that having established your true marketability and having a good handle on who you are and what you have to offer an employer, that you're in a much better position to start to think about pulling your CV together, if this is still relevant for you. Now is also the time to explore different types of jobs, careers and work you may have considered in the past but never had the courage to do anything about. In order to do this you need to be focused and set your priorities, as you can't do everything at once. By following the Cycle you will feel excited, motivated, confident and eager to explore opportunities and reinvent yourself!

You may by now have a clear idea of what's next for you, maybe a number of options you'd like to explore before you decide or you might still be totally in the dark. This is not uncommon. How advanced you are with your new thinking is not so important at this point. *So, what should you be doing at this stage? What are some of your options?*

Unravelling the clues

Having come this far you must now start to challenge what the output from all the exercises so far is telling you. Consider carefully how you can use this knowledge to determine your next step. First and foremost, revisit, reflect and review the key exercises from Chapters 1 to 3 because you may see things in a different light second time round. As previously mentioned, reflection and review are key components of the career transition process. To help you further unravel the clues, gain focus and clarity to move from the Darkness to the Light, you now need to:

- Get out there
- Meet people
- Research
- Network
- Challenge your thinking
- Dip a toe in the water
- Be opportunistic

✎ *Exercise - Pathway To The Future*

To help you move forward, let's look at some key questions you need to ask yourself:

	Question
1	(a) Do you still definitely want to be employed? (b) If so, do you know what type of job you would like to do yet?
2	Where might you apply your skills, attributes and values?
3	Have you thought about a particular company or organisation?

4	Does a particular type of environment or sector appeal?
5	(a) Are you still looking to progress your career? (b) If not what would 'downscaling' mean for you?
6	(a) Have you had enough of working for other people? (b) If so, do you like the thought of being your own boss and working for yourself?
7	If you start up your own business what can you do?
8	(a) Have you thought about changing the 'JOB' mindset altogether and considered a portfolio career? (b) How does changing your working lifestyle by deriving income from tapping into your talents, interests and passions appeal to you?

As you can see, these are some very big questions which you may well find quite daunting. However, I will guide you through the process, just as a set of traffic lights will take you safely across a major junction: to help you get the best out of this step of the Cycle, so you can move confidently onto step 5 and decide what to do.

But *What* To Do? *What* Approaches Are There?

At this stage of the Cycle there are three broad areas for you to consider.

1. To ensure you STOP making the most common mistakes

2. To consider some basic development options to get READY for a brighter future

3. To reflect on some simple points you can GO for now

(i) What To Avoid. STOP!

Impatience – Break things down into manageable chunks

It is only natural you will want to see results from your efforts so far. However, unless you have already come to some definite conclusions about what you want to do, until you have completed the next two steps of the Cycle it is unlikely you will see real progress. You have not yet started on the 'outer self' career development work to get to you to this point. A good strategy is to break tasks or activities down into bite size chunks so you can achieve 'small wins'. This is important to build momentum, keep you motivated and stay on track.

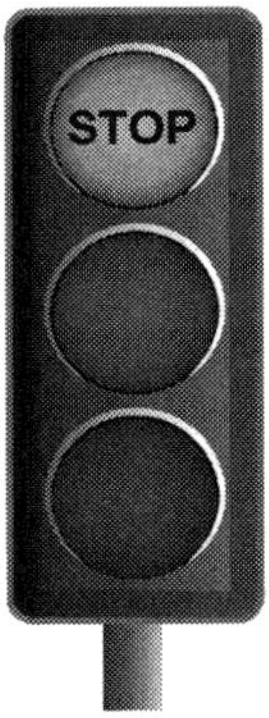

Sometimes you just need to 'be' rather than 'do'.

I find at this stage of the process, many people feel they need to be doing something proactive all the time towards their career change. What time you can allocate will clearly depend on your situation, as if you have a demanding professional or executive job, then you will need to make time around your busy schedule.

However, it is often when you aren't looking for anything in particular that you will suddenly experience and appreciate what is staring you in the face, rather than frantically building up and completing your 'to do' list. Less is often more and by slowing down your mind, your intuitive feelings and inner voice will often give you the insight you need.

'Being an extra in your own movie'

Another key mistake you might make at this stage of the process is to compromise and settle for second best. What do I mean by this? Essentially, if you are looking at a total career change or even a fairly similar job but in a different sector or environment, you can often make the mistake of underselling yourself and taking a lower level job on the basis of being new to the sector or the type of work. If you have been working on your change for some while, without making any real headway, you could be lacking in confidence or self-belief, so will be playing into the hands of an exploitative employer. You don't want to 'be an extra in your own movie', when you have the skills, talents, attributes etc. to play a starring role, do you?

All the work you've done around your true marketability should clearly highlight that you have much to offer, so never undersell yourself and instead aim your sights higher! Believe in your abilities, including being able to successfully reinvent yourself, so you can navigate your way to a brighter future. In setting your target or goal take heed of the following inspirational quote from Michelangelo, painter, sculptor, architect and poet (1475 – 1564): *"The greater danger for most of us is not that our aim is too high and we miss it, but that it is too low and we reach it."*.

Out of the frying pan into the fire!

What happens if while you are working through the Cycle process, you get headhunted for a similar opportunity to the job you are currently doing or have done before? Will you, like me, feel flattered and be tempted to jump at the first opportunity that comes along? However, now you have come this far, you may never get a better opportunity to reinvent yourself and redesign your career. Unless you really challenge yourself further to explore what might be possible, you could easily be jumping out of the frying pan into the fire and you don't want to get burnt, do you?

Just because you are good at something doesn't mean you enjoy it! *Along with a 'scattergun approach', thinking that you must continue to do work you are good at even if you don't really enjoy it, ranks as one of the most common mistakes that people make when considering their careers. This is something I learnt very early on my journey and it's a really important point to help you make a successful career change and end up doing work you love.*

Having completed the exercises in Chapter 3, you will have uncovered a number of things you are best at and you enjoy doing the most. Equally, you might uncover things you are best at but don't really enjoy. ***If so, now is the time to challenge yourself to consider whether you wish to continue with such work as your main job or at all, because you do have CHOICE!***

Not being true to yourself

It is often at this stage of the Cycle and the career transition process that you have a dawn of realisation that you are or were actually in the wrong job yourself. If *1 in 2 people is 'in the wrong job' and 2 out of 3 are 'unfulfilled'*, you could easily be a square peg in a round hole, especially if your situation has changed since you started reading this book? If you now feel you are, you don't want to continue in this vein and become increasingly unhappy do you? I have met so many people who just stuck at their jobs because it was easier to stay in their comfort zone with the knowledge that they could pay their bills each month. This might work for a while but at some point you will reach a peak of frustration and 'the volcano will erupt'!

Wouldn't it be great if you started to reframe and change your attitude so that you see things in a very different light?

I remember vividly a woman in one of my workshops, a number of years ago, suddenly blurted out *"You know what Steve, I now realise I've just wasted the last 20 years of my life"*. When I challenged her as to what she meant by such a controversial statement, she said she now realised she had been untrue to herself and she really hated the job and work she had been doing and was definitely a square peg in a round hole. She was another example of someone stuck in 'the velvet rut', but what an awakening! All is not lost - remember, *"You cannot recreate the past but you can create an exciting new future."*

I meet many people, especially from the IT and Finance sectors, who openly admit they only did the job because it paid well. This might serve your purpose for a number of years but as you get older, your values change, you will realise there is more to life than money, you face a source of constant and increasing frustration. **Be authentic, true to your values and you will discover fulfilment.**

Not being able to see past a different type of JOB

Working as a Career Coach, I now know there are very definitely many alternatives and you always have CHOICE. The reality is that the majority of people are conditioned to think and believe that career change still means they must have another job, because this is what they have had their entire career. However, as in my situation and with many of my clients, *'if you have been there, done that and got the tee shirt'*, maybe it's time to consign the old one to the bin and look for a totally different one? Instead, **consider whether you actually want another 'traditional' job at all?**

Don't let recruiters, 'head hunters' or other people control your future. Take control yourself and learn to become 'the architect of your own future'!

Many people fall into the trap of believing recruitment or executive search consultants will be their savior when making a career change, and then place great or even total reliance on such people. I once had a client in a career development workshop, whose proud boast was that he was signed up with nineteen different recruitment agencies. He was most upset when the general consensus of the group was that he was wasting his time! Depending on what jobs you are aspiring to, build relationships with industry specific recruiters and executive search consultants. **The key is to make sure they understand your true marketability and don't try to fit you into a box you have outgrown or no longer wish to be in.** However, as recruiters are all about finding the right fit for the hiring company or organisation, they will find it hard, if not impossible, to fit you into a new box that you have never been in before.

You must understand that their motivation is different from yours, because they work on high levels of commission for placing candidates. This means that if you are a hot prospect they will be 'all over you like the proverbial rash' and talk to you as if they are your best friend. Unfortunately, if they find more suitable candidates, they will drop you like a stone and suddenly become harder to find than the 'Scarlet Pimpernel'. Recruitment consultants are part of the job search mix but like everything, there are good and bad. Learn to manage them rather than the other way round. I have developed a brilliant relationship with an executive search consultant who shares my values and business ethos. He always goes the extra mile and is happy to share his knowledge and experience to benefit his potential candidates, which is rarely the case. He has also taken the trouble to understand how I can support some of his candidates who are 'lost in their jobs', in transition or just need to rethink their careers. Therefore, if you do find a really good recruitment or executive search consultant they can play a part in 'finding your gold'. However, the reality is you are highly unlikely to achieve a successful career change by relying on recruitment consultants. Always remember that **only you** can take full responsibility for your successful career change.

(ii) What To Consider: ***GET READY***

There are a number of development opportunities worth pursuing that would not only help improve your skills but also enhance your ability to change careers. Depending on your current situation and whether you have left your job or not, you can gain great benefits from volunteering, work experience, work shadowing, secondments or redeployment, especially leading or being part of project teams.

Being able to utilise and maximize your existing skills, learn new skills, prove your value to a new team or project can provide a real sense of purpose and feeling valued. By dipping a toe in the water and taking advantage of these opportunities you give yourself an excellent platform to build from, something different and live on your CV (if this was unpaid work, you don't need to say so on your CV as you can show it as a short project) from which it becomes much easier to secure a different type of job or determine what you want to do next. By having a positive experience you will also give yourself a big confidence boost!

The Power of Volunteering or Work Experience

If you have already left your job or you are returning to work following a career break, as part of your career transition journey and to help explore opportunities, volunteering or 'work experience' can be excellent ways to dip a toe in the water to see if you enjoy a particular type of job. If you are still employed you can volunteer for a secondment, or else find opportunities outside the organisation to dip a toe in the water at weekends or by taking a couple of days leave. These opportunities may include working within a particular company or a totally different work environment, e.g. an outdoor job instead of an office job, or a sales job instead of a back office support role. If you think that by volunteering you are just being exploited and you find yourself only focusing on the fact that you are working for nothing, reframe your thinking. I have worked with many clients for whom this approach has completely changed their perception and been the catalyst for achieving their successful career transition and change. So, what have you got to lose?

Victoria Pendleton, the legendary British female cyclist, retired from competitive cycling in 2012, after a glittering career, including winning many Olympic and World Championship Gold medals. When asked what she will do next her response was *"I have only been focused on my final Olympic goal. Now this is over, I will start to think about what I can do next and will look at doing some work experience to find out what I like"*. Shortly after this she became a candidate for the BBC's popular TV programme 'Strictly Come Dancing' and swapped her gold medal for gold sequins. A bold move and a risk, but one wondered what opportunities this 'experience' might present for her in the future. She has since moved on to combine her love of competitive sport with horses and become an amateur jockey, which could no doubt lead her to eventually turning professional, or part of a portfolio career.

The following case study is a brilliant example of someone who really has 'become the architect of their own future', the philosophy of this book. Jacqui's story illustrates how finding 'work experience opportunities', coupled with following the complete six step Career Navigation Cycle process can transform your life.

Jacqui's Story

When I first started working with Jacqui by her own admission, she was *'lost in the fog'*. She had been a very successful IT Director in a global corporation but was clearly not passionate about IT and had lost interest in the industry and the corporate arena. It was definitely time for a complete career and lifestyle change. Having started life in the Police force, her career had evolved by accident rather than design. She had known instinctively when the time was right to break out into the commercial world. Now, she was keen to explore new opportunities in tune with her values, passions and interests, as she had gained a huge amount from Steps 1-3 of the Cycle.

When it came to exploring specific opportunities, like many people, she drew a blank. However, in reviewing some of her passions and interests, there were recurring themes around her interest in gardening, nurturing plants and flowers and maybe even setting up her own garden nursery. Jacqui admitted that she was prone to procrastination and knew she had to keep building momentum, so explored the possibility of getting work experience in a garden centre. She quickly found a contact, a manager of a local garden centre, who was keen to help and in no time she was 'in amongst it' and loving it!

The outcome: realisation that running a garden centre is a big commitment and maybe was better as a longer term objective. Moreover, if she became the owner, she would employ a manager to run the garden centre for her. Due to a back injury Jacqui struggled with some of the heavy work. However, she realised that there were lots of other lighter jobs and ways to earn money from her love of plants and gardening.

When I last saw Jacqui she had decided what to do and had taken positive action to set up a small hanging basket business, with a view to building other income streams in tandem. She had also signed up to a year-long horticultural course to gain a formal qualification, whilst also getting hands-on experience in another garden centre environment. Her work experience had proved to be invaluable. She was really happy and was now well and truly on the way to making a successful career change and doing work she loved, also with a longer term vision for the future.

Work Shadowing

Work shadowing is another very useful option that allows you to 'dip a toe' in the water to see whether a particular type of job the job, career, company or an alternative environment is right for you. This is particularly helpful if you are still employed and don't have much spare time, as you may only need to do this for a day or so, or a few hours here and there, working around your job commitments.

There are a couple of good examples that spring to mind that demonstrate the benefits of work shadowing in determining what you want to do once you have successfully completed Steps 1-3.

Firstly there was a client who wanted to explore the possibility of setting up their own café or coffee shop. It may well be that various TV shows have influenced people to think that it would be cool to run their own café, as I have had a number of clients and friends who have considered this option. My client had been having discussions with a member of the family, who was running a café in a different part of the country, as he was interested in doing the same. He agreed to take a few days off work to visit family and spend time work shadowing, to see first-hand what it was like to run a café before he did any further research.

This turned out to be an excellent strategy, as he knew after only a few hours that such a venture was not for him. "Why? Because... he had not anticipated a number of factors that were required to make the venture a success, i.e. the work was highly physical and also placed great demands on personal time and finances. Aside of these demands, he had discovered it was a highly competitive market and not easy to make a good living. Certainly not a wasted trip as such a venture was something he could now rule out. He also was now much more aware of some of his skills and attributes he did want to use but in a very different environment.

The second example relates to an IT Director from the corporate world who had become disenchanted with large corporations as a result of their constant rounds of restructuring. He wanted to continue to use his high level IT skills, knowledge and experience, but in a different environment where he would be truly valued. I encouraged him to change his mindset and rethink his strategy. He decided he didn't want to make a complete career change but to instead change tactics and explore whether working for a small company, where he would have much greater autonomy, would work for him.

He researched companies within easy commuting distance, establishing the names of the managing director and chief executive. Next he made targeted, speculative approaches explaining his situation and his objective, in a very positive way. This proved very successful, opening up opportunities with a couple of small businesses who agreed to him doing some work shadowing. He quickly established he would thrive working for a smaller business and in an environment where he could really make a difference and be true to his values. The result: one of the companies recognised his true marketability and offered him an excellent role which he was delighted to accept.

Changing Career Within Your Organisation – Secondments and Redeployment

Although this book is primarily focused on 'winning through career change' and leaving your organisation to move into a totally different career, for some people it may be preferable to consider an interim step by undertaking an alternative role within your existing organisation.

"How do you do this?" I hear you ask. Well there are two main ways of approaching the situation:

1. Secondment.

This is the *temporary* transfer to another position to undertake a completely different role elsewhere within the organisation – it can be locally or wider within the organisation, even to a different country. Notably, it may also be possible to move across local authority organisations in the public sector with mutual agreement.

Secondments could be advertised but more often you will need to be proactive and instigate discussions with your line manager on the basis of your ongoing development needs and broadening your skillset. To make a compelling case, you will need to focus on the mutual benefits, not just for you but also the organisation.

In terms of exploring opportunities, one of the main benefits of secondments is that they are usually for a fixed period, although they might be extended by mutual consent. This will give you plenty of time to establish whether any such new role is the right next step for your career.

As secondments are only of a temporary nature, it helps to be proactive, whilst you are in the role and thinking about your next step. You might otherwise be disappointed when an enjoyable assignment comes to an end that there is no permanent post for you to move into and you must then return to your original post.

Secondments can provide you with invaluable experience, new knowledge and skills that will enable you to add some new and impressive information to your CV to immediately make you more marketable. Also, you will have a much greater chance of being able to secure a similar role either within or outside of your organisation in the future.

2. Redeployment.

This process usually gives permanent employees, whose jobs are at risk of redundancy, the chance to find a new job. It can occasionally be used in other circumstances when it becomes necessary to move an individual away from a particular work area, but unlike secondments, rarely is it used on request.

Redeployment more commonly arises as part of a major restructuring or reorganisation, and the employer has an obligation to help find suitable alternative employment. Depending upon other vacancies elsewhere within the organisation, the placement could again be either locally or anywhere within the organisation.

A key point to bear in mind with this process is that there is usually some form of 'matching process' used to optimise an individual's skills and experience, so you are unlikely to be matched and placed in jobs that you are not suitable for. However, there is no guarantee of redeployment into an identical type of role or specialism as matches may be based on your general knowledge, skills and experience. Therefore you could be matched to a different role in an entirely different section or department, where the role would be considered of similar or equal value.

Redeployment is inevitably a stressful situation, as it difficult for you to influence the outcome. However, by being flexible, positive and keeping an open mind, you could start on a new career path whilst securing continuity of employment, rather than facing redundancy. I have known many people who have reluctantly moved into new roles actually discover that it gave them a new perspective and lease of life.

This is where being aware of your true marketability really helps as you could have a great opportunity to learn and develop into a new career and specialism - which in the longer term may lead to promotion in your new field. Equally, as with secondments, by taking on such a new challenge and making a success of this, you will increase your marketability and your chances to later successfully change your career outside of your organisation.

Joe's Story

This is an interesting case study about Joe. He epitomises the very sentiment of 'dipping a toe in the water'. He worked in a senior Operational role but was extremely unhappy and looking for options to do something different. He was by his own admission a square peg in a round hole, unfulfilled, stressed and frustrated, which was affecting his health. Although he was responsible for managing a small team of people, Joe was never comfortable managing people and all the challenges this presents, not least of meeting targets, poor performance, absenteeism, conflict and his values were at odds with his job, although he believed in the values of the organisation.

He eventually left the organisation but initially was in the 'fog" and unclear about what to do next. By coaching Joe through the Cycle and establishing his true marketability, it became increasingly evident that Joe thrived when solving challenging problems by creatively using computer software. Joe enjoyed managing 'things', especially technology, rather than people! Joe had the realisation that there may be an alternative to the pressure of being made operationally responsible for achieving targets. He therefore considered the possibility of moving into a completely different role in another location elsewhere within the organisation. This would allow him to be responsible for providing the data rather than managing the data himself.

Because he understood both sides of the business, he was brilliantly well placed to know what information was required and how best to present this to enable senior managers to easily identify and then tackle the performance issues to achieve their key operational targets. Surely a 'win-win' situation? Yes, except that although Joe was a wizard with technology, he wasn't 'formally qualified' to undertake such a role. The answer… utilising his networks to initially do a day's work shadowing to see first-hand the end-to-end process of how the key data was being compiled. He then went on to secure work experience for a few weeks in a similar role elsewhere, to gain direct experience that would allow him to decide if this career change was really for him.

The result... Joe proved to be a shining star and was snapped up for some initial project work on a temporary contract. Having worked through the Cycle and gained clarity, Joe followed through and achieved his desired career goal. He is now back full-time with the organisation. Joe is now doing work he excels in and enjoys. This outcome was of great benefit both to Joe and the organisation ...an all-round great result!

When at Step 4 and exploring opportunities, it is inevitable that you may well be ruling out different types of work, jobs or business opportunities as much as ruling them in. Don't be disheartened as this may allow you to find out what you want to do or wish to pursue further.

This is not a setback, but a positive way of testing the situation - much like Thomas Edison when each failed attempt to invent the light bulb was a further step towards achieving success and the end goal.

This said, remember it is important to focus your energy and set your intent on what you do want, rather than what you don't want. Joe clearly did just this, he knew what he didn't want anymore, worked through what might be possible, set his positive intent, networked his way to explore a new opportunity, dipped a toe in the water and took positive action to win through his career change, as you can too.

More on all of these aspects to follow, so read on.

(iii) What To Embrace Now. **GO!**

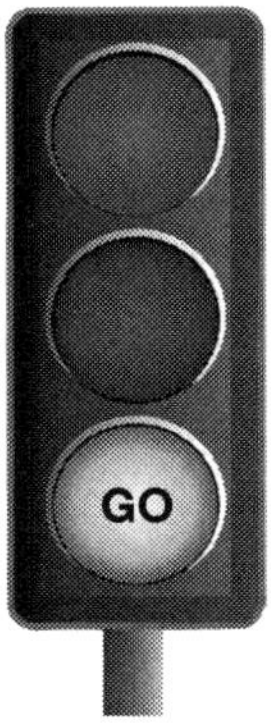

What other approach can you adopt now?

Although it is alien to most people to even think it, one of the first considerations is **do you actually want another job i.e. an employed role?** Now is the time to challenge yourself and step out of your comfort zone. If you are looking to change career consider what opportunities this can really open up. Remember, you do have CHOICE!

Listen to your inner voice – follow your gut!

In Chapter 1 I talked about your inner voice. As a result of my experiences job searching, with recruiters, my 'scattergun approach' and negative interview experiences, my inner voice was niggling away at me asking the same questions over and over:

- What are you doing?
- Why are you putting yourself through this awful job search process?
- Why are you going to these interviews?
- Do you really want the job anyway?
- Do you really want to travel so far to work every day?
- Do you want to spend your life commuting daily on horrendous motorways or in constant traffic jams?
- Is there another option?
- Do you want to work for another boss?
- Do you really want another job at all?
- Why don't you become your own boss?
- What do you really want out of life?

So many questions and so few answers! Do **you** recognise any of these thoughts? If so, I empathise. Don't make the same mistakes I initially did by letting your head rule your heart. Instead, embrace what your instincts, values and passions are telling you.

Be bold

Challenging yourself on the questions coming from your inner voice to follow your gut instincts, can help you open up a whole new way of thinking. You can rule out work you may no longer be interested in doing, whilst gaining more clarity about what you do enjoy and what to focus on.

In my last employed role, I was Rewards & Benefits Manager in my Company. Everyone said: *"You're really good at this stuff Steve, great at designing pay schemes, developing benefits initiatives, incentive schemes and all this associated activity."* Did I enjoy it? I enjoyed the end result, I enjoyed seeing the results of my efforts and the impact it had on the company and benefits to all the staff. Being true to myself and looking from a different perspective, there was a lot of boring, mundane work including number crunching and analysis which is just not me. I quickly came to the conclusion that I didn't want to continue with the Reward and Benefits work on a full-time basis. It was time to change and move on. This was another career defining moment for me and I only did such work as a part of my portfolio career when I started my business, which I will cover in Chapter 5. If you also feel this way about the work you have done previously then be bold and move on and reap the benefits.

Focus on what you want – intent

Thinking back to The Law of Attraction, one of the most important aspects of this is focusing on what you **do** want rather than what you **don't** want. Although, as already mentioned, it is helpful to rule things out and it is often easier to do so at this stage, by focusing heavily on what you don't want you will probably manifest just this. It is so important to remember you are what you think and feel. Therefore, focus your energy wholeheartedly on achieving what you do want. Think about your intent and focus on this and I'm sure you will find this much more energising. Clear out your negative thinking and review some of the work you have done already around your success criteria; the Values, Needs, Skills, Attributes and Motivated Abilities you fleshed out which are likely to provide clues here.

If you are still unclear on what it is you do want, and many people do get stuck on this, you need to set your intent to *'I want to know what I want'*. Although this may seem somewhat strange, by setting and focusing on this desire, you will begin attracting information, you will begin attracting people and opportunity; you will begin attracting many things to select from. Over time, from the steady stream of ideas that will flow your way, you will get a better idea of what you specifically desire. There are many books and resources which explain this amazing law of the universe. *'The Secret' (Rhonda Byrne)* is without doubt the most well-known. It has become a cult book and film, having achieved worldwide success and recognition, especially after Oprah Winfrey dedicated a complete TV show to it.

'The Missing Secret' is also an excellent audio programme (CD/MP3 etc.) from Dr Joe Vitale, which focuses on the Law of Attraction in a big way. Joe Vitale was also featured in the film of 'The Secret' but he felt, as good as the book and film were, there was a missing link. This is around the aspect of 'clearing', which I have alluded to in terms of clearing out your negative thinking. He also covers in more depth the importance of taking positive action, which we will explore in Chapter 6.

I have only come to understand and see firsthand the power of The Law of Attraction, since I immersed myself in Personal Development. I could also see the strong link and benefits to Career Development, especially at key times of change in life, such as changing careers. As with the Cycle, it is important to believe in the process. Your positive thoughts and emotions will generate positive energy to let the universe take care of the rest!

Keep an open mind

While you are exploring opportunities, you may make definite decisions, as with some of the examples, but you will be more likely to be ruling things in or out as you research. Therefore, it is important to keep an open mind. Ideas will often come to you in the most unlikely moments and can be triggered by conversations with people, something you see or read and I certainly would like to think from this book. Capture your thoughts somewhere you can easily find them, as you never know when they will come home to roost!

Core belief

As I mentioned in Chapter 2, ***"If your WHY is strong enough the WHAT and HOW will follow"***. To explain this statement, if your sense of purpose and why you want to change career, be your own boss or downscale your career is strong enough, the specific what you do next and how you will achieve it will follow. This is all part of your career transition journey and the Cycle process, so **you must be patient and go with the flow.** Don't be tempted to take short cuts. Keep following the process to win through!

Become a detective

By becoming a detective I do not mean you should consider a career with the Criminal Investigations Department. Become adept at researching and sourcing key information to help you evaluate potential jobs, work or careers plus learning where to find useful information. Explore a variety of websites, reference books, professional associations, online forums and through the development of new contacts who can steer you in the right direction.

Visualise your goal

If you already have your end goal in mind, e.g. setting up your own business but are unsure in what area, as with your 'vision of success exercise', you can cut out pictures to make a collage or draw something that represents your vision. Writing down key statements will give you constant daily focus. Alternatively, you may find online vision boards, such as Pinterest, more powerful. These are also a great way of piecing together ideas to help shape your future. For those of you who are very visual, visualising your goals is an effective strategy to help open up your thinking and explore new opportunities.

Visualisation is a fantastic skill which can help you achieve many positive outcomes for the rest of your life. Like learning any new skill, visualising takes practice and discipline but you will reap the rewards if you persevere.

Dr Lee Pulos is a renowned Guru in the art of visualisation. His audio book, *'The Power of Visualisation – Seeing is Achieving'* is recognised to be one of the best reference materials on this subject.

Developing your CV, bios and profiles

You now have enough information to start building a powerful CV in a very different way than you would have done previously. Instead of focusing on a CV to do more of the same, you can now use the much of the information you have gleaned from your true marketability coupled with understanding your values and needs. It is not the purpose of this book to focus in great detail on how to write a good CV as there are dozens of such books available, together with a plethora of online information. However, it is important at this stage to ensure you really flesh out the key information from the exercises in Chapters 2 and 3, which will help you stand out from the crowd.

The key is **you must bring yourself to life** on all your paper and electronic marketing materials, e.g. CV, bios and online profiles to best promote and enhance your personality, character traits, attitude, work ethic, key skills and achievements. In two pages of quality information, make sure your true marketability and personal brand shine through. Your key objective from creating a compelling CV is to give a potential employer a great reason to invite you to an interview and it will also put you in good stead for any volunteering, work experience or work shadowing opportunities. Although it may seem obvious, in a nutshell, your CV is to get you on the interview 'yes' pile, yet many people forget this!

Let's look at how you achieve this objective, as what I am about to share with you is unlikely to be written this way in any other CV reference material but it works!

- The first key point is your CV is not written for you but for a potential employer so it must excite them
- Consider your CV must pass two tests to be in with a chance: the '10 second' and the *'So What?'* tests
- The first half page must compel the reader within 10 seconds to want to review the remainder of your CV
- The *'So What?'* test challenges the inclusion of typical bland and often unsubstantiated statements you may have made about your skills, attributes or experience
- Most people's CV's have these, so your task is to restructure and rephrase such statements, like the example on the next page
- Use positive language that focuses on your work achievements, contribution, skills and outcomes
- You are providing evidence of your competency, rather than what you have done

An example: skills statements should be one sentence and clearly contextualised, e.g. *"Excellent report writing skills producing meaningful executive summaries for Boards to make informed strategic decisions."* Isn't it clear that this is very different to just saying 'excellent report writing skills' which most people would do, but doesn't pass the 'so what test'? With such a specific statement, I'm sure you would rather ask this candidate to an interview, wouldn't you?

Likewise, it pays to have monetary amounts, percentages, timescales and any other tangible measures to highlight achievements, especially in relation to improvements or cost savings. By taking this approach, you will also have some excellent ammunition for interviews!

Dino's Story

Although Dino worked at a high level in Sales & Marketing, he was the classic example of somebody who could sell 'ice to the Eskimos' but couldn't sell himself. Before we started working together, Dino had signed up to a large career management consultancy and invested a significant amount of money. Unfortunately, despite his investment, after many months he was getting nowhere with his job search. Why? Simply because he hadn't done any of the 'inner self' work in Steps 1-3 of the Cycle, so he was at sea. Criminal really but that's another story. Consequently, Dino was blissfully unaware of what he had to offer, his very definite Values and Needs or his strong Personal Brand. As a result, his CV wasn't focused, targeted nor selling him in anything like the best light. He was pitching for the wrong jobs with no real strategy, based on his desire to land a new job quickly, instead of exploring in more depth what the job entailed and whether these jobs were in tune with his Values and Needs. Another classic example of a scattergun approach!

The solution: we had to go back to square one and once he had completed Steps 1-3 of the Cycle, Dino gained real focus and clarity. I then worked with him on his CV, which had been way too upmarket and 'flowery', to become a true representation of him (very genial and down to earth) and really brought him to life. Now his CV was very targeted and focused, he started receiving interest from companies and was able to sell himself confidently at interviews. The end result: Dino was in the enviable position of having two job offers. He based his decision on his Values & Needs, landed a fantastic job that he loved, which has proved mutually beneficial for him and his company and proved to also be an excellent launch pad to progress his career.

Be Opportunistic - Speculative Applications

Something I constantly encourage my clients to be aware of is the importance of both spotting and creating opportunities. For instance, you may see a job advertised which you feel is not right for you, but you like the sound of the employer and maybe the environment. In such situations try the following approach:

- Contact the recruiting manager if they have one and not the HR department, as this can often be a 'black hole'
- Always establish the name of the recruiting line manager and target them personally either by telephone or email, as 'to whom it may concern', never works!
- Explain you have seen the vacancy advertised, you like the sound of the company but are interested in a different or maybe higher level role with more responsibilities

- Sound positive and enthusiastic and genuinely interested, as your tone of voice will be a giveaway!

Our daughter landed a brilliant management job by taking exactly this approach, as the advertised vacancy was a level below what she was seeking. She liked the sound of the company and they liked her. Consequently, once they had secured suitable funding they offered her the job opportunity she really wanted. So again this was a mutually beneficial win-win situation.

The same speculative approach can be taken if there are specific companies you wish to target that are not currently advertising vacancies. What is the worst that can happen? Being told there are no vacancies for your level? Instead, they may take your details and ask you to email your CV to keep on file. However, I have worked with many people who have turned such opportunities into job roles. The company was considering a similar role and the application helped to crystallise the need. As with many things in life, you can often be in the right place at the right time but to a large extent you create your own luck, which is very useful when changing careers!

Turning around unsuccessful job interviews

Although it is understandable that you will be disappointed when you receive a negative response to a job interview, I have often seen how you can turn this negative into a positive. A short, polite and professional email to the key decision maker stating how much you enjoyed the interview, maybe the environment, what you heard about the company and their plans and how you would be interested in similar opportunities, can often pay dividends. Be bold - why would you not want to do this?

The most fantastic example I can recall was a woman who did exactly as I've highlighted. Much to her surprise, she received a phone call out of the blue a few months later from the company concerned. It transpired that the successful applicant had decided to relocate abroad and having been impressed by the enthusiasm and initiative she showed, they immediately contacted her to see if she was still available and interested in the job. Although she had a short term contract and was exploring other opportunities, nothing concrete had emerged at this stage. She agreed to meet them again on the basis that if they still liked each other, the job was hers. Everything went to plan. Only the outcome was even better. The company had won a new contract in Singapore and they asked her to head it up for them. As she was single and mobile, this was a dream come true as it was the perfect career and life change! Therefore the key lessons here are:

- Be true to your values
- Apply for the right jobs
- Be opportunistic
- Be bold
- Be positive with your initial approach and any follow up

As you have done much of the hard work already by revisiting your values and needs you will now see much more clearly what jobs, companies or opportunities are right for you.

How To Avoid 'Walking In Treacle'

In this section we will be examining some of the areas that hold us back, where we get stuck and prevented from progressing and moving forward. Often when changing careers, although some progress is made it can feel like going 'two steps forward and one step back' and this can give rise to a growing sense of frustration, disillusionment and disappointment, often likened to 'walking in treacle'. But I will now offer you some ways to overcome this debilitating condition.

Face Your FEARS

In Chapter 1, we looked at facing your fears. At this stage when you're exploring opportunities, do you find this is where you are now openly facing your fears as well? This is often the point where reality kicks in for many people, so keep reading, following the Cycle and enjoy your journey. Now is a good time to revisit the two acronyms for "fear" in Chapter 1, which have really helped to change many people's perception about what "fear" really is. Sportsmen and performers will always want to get pumped up and get their adrenalin going before a big event. This is a key time of change for you, a key stage of the Career Navigation Cycle and transition process, so exploring opportunities and making your breakthrough is a big event for you, too, so your emotions will be high. Ask yourself the question:

Is your *'fear'* related to feeling *'excitement and anticipation'*? In which case this is positive? Or is your *'fear'* based on your beliefs that maybe you *'can't change'* or you are still *'fearful'* for other negative reasons?"

The solution: you need to **give yourself permission** to express your fears, so you can face them. This way you can learn to reframe your fears and banish them, as we covered previously. For many people, giving themselves permission to express and work on their fears using the two acronyms from the exercise, is all that you need to change your perceptions. Try it and see how you get on. By the time you complete the book and the six Steps of the Cycle you will be ready to move from 'fearful to fearless'. Don't worry if you aren't there yet, as you are still a work in progress and you will get there, won't you?

Pauline's Story

Pauline is one of our top executive clients. Although she had taken the decision to leave her employer, after many years, she had difficulty letting go and leaving her past employed career behind. Like Jane, who is featured in Chapter 1, she had major concerns about whether she could be successful in her own right, running her own consultancy. How on earth would she make it work? These questions come up time and time again for so many people:

- "Why would anyone want to pay me to do that?"
- "There are so many other people out there, why would they want to pay me?"

My answer is always the same: "People were very happy to pay you for many years in your career previously so why would they not want to pay you now?" You've proved that you're an expert in your field and you have many other great skills and attributes, so you can do the same by changing career and running your own business. Again, it's a shift of mindset. Once you realise and understand this, it's absolutely no different. In Pauline's case, she was considering undertaking a PhD in Performance Management and harboured a fear of "How is this going to work?" or "Will I be accepted? etc. As always this has proved to be an unfounded fear. Pauline never looked back, having developed a successful consultancy with some great projects and clients and especially enjoying her freedom and independence.

If You Are Returning To Work Following A Career Break - Use Your Time Productively

One size does not fit all. Therefore there is no absolute right way to spend your time while in career transition, if you are looking to return to work following a career break. However, as you can now see there are many options to help you explore opportunities. Whatever you do, try to avoid 'knee jerk' reactions to situations just because you think you should.

I've met many people over the years who were very disciplined. They got up at the same time as when they were employed and then spent an "eight hour working day keeping busy" doing as many activities as possible. However, this is often not the right approach. Spending hours every day on the Internet job searching is definitely not the most productive use of your time. It can be hugely demoralising, isolating and incredibly time consuming. But why do people do this? Mostly because it appears to be the easiest option, seems the right thing to do and it gives them a feeling of being productive.

The reality is that you are:

- Putting yourself in amongst all the competition
- Not giving yourself an opportunity to explore new avenues or really test the water for what might be possible in a new career
- If you are returning to work and changing careers, it is highly unlikely you will win through by spending your time online looking at different types of jobs

One of the biggest negatives for many people is facing the risk of multiple rejections and the equally frustrating 'black hole syndrome', where your applications disappear never having seen the light of day. What can be even worse is not getting responses at all. Being left hanging, not knowing, can be even more frustrating than getting a rejection.

All this frustration and angst can really knock the stuffing out of you, in turn knocking your confidence and motivation, just when you need it the most. Therefore, you need to reframe your thinking because, although your job applications are of utmost importance to you, employers' priorities will be completely different and as annoying as this is, you have to respect this. Importantly, the issue here isn't about procrastination and intentionally creating delay, it is about spending your time wisely and focusing on the *right* things. Whilst I admit and empathise that being out of work is unlikely to give you the same self-motivation as being in work, you do need to feel that you are being productive and achieving something.

To focus your mind, consider - *what is the consequence and value of what I am doing right now?* This is a great way to decide whether you are spending your time wisely and productively on activities that are beneficial and will move you towards your end goal. If not, you have to question the validity of what you are doing and move onto something that will be more productive. Consider, when are you at your best? Organising your day around when you are most energised and focused makes a lot of sense. This way you will know when is best to get stuck into key activities, e.g. researching, job search, rewriting your CV, developing your online profile and networks. Likewise you will know when to take some downtime and just 'be'.

Energy Boosters And Drainers

In this difficult transition phase, especially when you are exploring opportunities, it is really helpful to know what gives you a much needed energy boost. Equally, consider what you should avoid, what has a negative impact on you and will drain your energy.

Let's look back to some of the pointers in Chapter 1, to help boost your energy:

- Surround yourself with positive people
- Consult personal development books, audio material (CDs, MP3s), films and downloads
- Attend motivational seminars and webinars

These activities can also be a great source of motivation and inspiration. Like me, I have a number of clients who have met likeminded people at workshops and seminars and they have either become great contacts, friends and sounding boards or they have even teamed up to work on projects or set up in businesses together.

Audio material is excellent for playing in the car especially when you are stuck in traffic, on journeys to family, friends or an interview. Brian Tracy makes reference to this and talks about using your car as *'a university on wheels'*. I have a client who now only listens to personal development CDs/MP3s whenever he is in his car. The impact on him has been remarkable, as he now feeds off the positive energy. He has turned his business and life around. Learning from personal development books, audio material and films means you grow personally, not academically, which will put you in much greater shape to tackle the challenges ahead for the rest of your life. I'm sure you will agree that this can only be of positive benefit to you.

For many people, going for walks, running or doing some form of exercise provides the necessary energy boost, but again everyone is different, so you must do what works for you. Sometimes it pays you to just *'be'* rather than *'do'*, so whatever helps you achieve this state, will give you the space to open up new thinking. Conversely, anything that has the reverse effect and becomes an energy drainer, you need to turn round to negate the impact e.g. too much isolation can often create negative thinking and mindset, which is often one of the biggest causes of procrastination.

✎ *Exercise – Recruit Yourself And Winning with Attitude*

Now is an appropriate time to review your Skills, Motivated Abilities and Attributes from previous exercises. Consider which are your top ten Skills and Attributes/Attitudinal aspects which will make the difference to win through career change and achieve your life goals. You can use these for self-marketing and to focus your energy to bring about your desired outcomes.

	Attitudes/Attributes	Skills
1		
2		
3		
4		
5		
6		
7		
8		
9		
10		

The Power And Value Of Social Media

The Growth Of Social Media

With the growth of Social Media has come the importance of having an online brand and presence. A good online profile or bio can make all the difference to you being found by the right people. The power of Social Media is the fact that you can talk to *so many people so quickly* when to do so face to face would take weeks and months. As highlighted in Chapter 1, everyone needs to embrace Social Media as an effective form of communication and to develop your online brand, whether you are running your own business or whether you are a serious professional in your specific business sector.

LinkedIn

LinkedIn (www.linkedin.com) is the professional version of Facebook. Although there are numerous imitations, LinkedIn is accepted as **the place** where professional people meet. It is estimated there are now over 400 million registered members with more than 2 new members joining every second. You could say it is rather like a market place or shopping mall where you can have access to a huge number of potential connections, information and also jobs to help you in your career quest. Therefore, use LinkedIn as your main business social network to develop your profile, online brand and presence, so you can be found and you can find and network with others. Getting quality recommendations for your profile and likewise giving quality recommendations for your valued and trusted connections can give you real kudos. Also, gaining a significant number of endorsements for the skills you now want to be recognised for (50+ is good and 99+ is great!) will help you stand out from the crowd.

LinkedIn has literally hundreds if not thousands of different online groups related to a huge variety of different sectors and business disciplines. These groups are a great way to learn about the latest trends, share knowledge and experience and develop your network with like-minded people. By getting involved in the many discussion forums, you also have a great opportunity to position yourself as an expert. Raising your profile in this way, will prompt people to look at your profile and, if they like what they see, they could well contact you to connect or possibly regarding potential jobs or self-employed opportunities.

As you are looking at a career change, explore the different types of groups in your field of interest before you decide which ones to join. Sometimes people put postings on such groups asking for thoughts on the best way to transition into particular jobs or careers in specific sectors, e.g. Charity sector. Again, this is an excellent way to show that you are in the market and get your name across and be noticed.

As mentioned early in Chapter 1, it is important to embrace the technological changes that are happening around us and LinkedIn is likely to be one of the most important to you, regardless of whether you wish to be employed or self-employed. By ignoring LinkedIn you do so at your peril, as you are cutting off one of the most important community and communication channels. Also, LinkedIn is now the first port of call for many recruiters and employers when looking for new talent or to fill vacancies, many of which might never be advertised or if so only on LinkedIn. Follow the adage 'you need to be in it to win it'. If you are concerned about how to set up your profile or get the best out of LinkedIn and this is holding you back, you can research this quite easily to find numerous tutorials on YouTube, LinkedIn itself as well as other websites and general blog postings. This is another opportunity where you can seek help from family, friends or utilise your networks of contacts who are already using the site effectively to help you get started or improve the way you already use LinkedIn.

Facebook

Although most people associate Facebook (www. facebook. com) with purely personal social activity, the general networking principle is wonderfully illustrated by a woman who attended one of my career transition workshops a few years ago. Having explained the importance of both offline and online networking and the power of social media, she declared that her best friend had just got her most recent job through Facebook! I noticed the quizzical looks from the other delegates, so asked her to explain to the group how her friend had achieved this.

It transpired that her friend had messaged out to her friends on Facebook, stating 'she was exploring new opportunities in her chosen field and did anyone know of any contacts they could put her in touch with?' She received two responses, one of whom invited her to a meeting and she got the job straightaway. The timescale - only two weeks from start to finish! Compare this with the average job application, which can take anything from one month to well over three months.

What this woman did was no different to phoning or meeting with a number of close contacts to achieve the same goal. However, the difference was in the speed of the whole process, which cannot be understated. This is the power of using your networks on Social Media. It is not just about reaching out to your connections; it is their connections that may help to unlock the key to your future. Equally importantly, she also bypassed the traditional recruitment process, which we will look at shortly.

Be careful how you manage your reputation on Facebook

One of my clients, a company director, shared a story with me about one of their employees, who worked with mainly black and minority ethnic colleagues and who had his Facebook page plastered with politically incorrect images and racist comments. He was identified as a company PR disaster waiting to happen and was duly sacked.

Unwittingly some people may choose to post 'racy' photos on their Facebook pages and, although these might be considered by some to be fun at the time, potential employers can access these when investigating candidates simply by using any search engine, such as Google. Unless you are going into modelling, keep such photos and your Facebook status 'private', so only your personal connections can see them otherwise you are asking for trouble. The same applies to people who inadvertently show drunken exploits to the world. There have even been cases of employees taking a 'sickie' and then posting about their hangover on Facebook and subsequently getting sacked! Make sure only the people you want to see these can, or seriously consider whether you should have them on Facebook at all.

Twitter

Unless you have become an avid tweeter, you are unlikely to know what all the fuss is about and why Twitter (https://twitter.com) has become an integral part of many people's daily lives. Apart from the main use for quick fire instant messages of maximum 140 characters and general chit chat, Twitter has become a useful search engine tool in its own right. In addition, the main benefit of Twitter is that it is yet another way for you to build your online presence and personal or company brand, when you use it as a marketing tool. Using Twitter as a way to develop your personal brand can be very effective. You can quickly open up new communication channels, participate in conversations and send regular 'micro blogs', which in turn will help you develop a new community to position you as an expert in your chosen new field, whether you wish to be employed or start your own business. As Twitter is a global social media tool, as with LinkedIn, by using it tactically and sharing lots of useful nuggets of information, you could open up unexpected new opportunities. One thing is certain, Twitter will evolve and change in ways that you should aim to keep abreast of, so if you don't get involved now, keep an open mind when you change your career.

Blogs

Whereas Twitter is focused on short, sharp blasts of specific, often daily or more regular communications, a blog is basically a journal that is available on the web. It can be anything from daily to ad hoc regularity. Blogs are more like personalised web sites where you use 'your voice' (or your business voice) to share knowledge, expertise and interesting information to get you or your business noticed. Blogs are also an excellent way of positioning yourself as a thought leader in your area of specialism or interest and to build your personal or business brand.

The really great news is that LinkedIn now has a brilliant publishing option. Therefore, if you enjoy writing about things you are passionate or knowledgeable about or you want to test the water to see how you get on with blogging, start by using LinkedIn publishing. It is a simple and fantastic way of getting noticed! This is especially true if what you publish will help others, challenge people's thinking or create intrigue. LinkedIn publishing has now become a brilliant vehicle for many people to publish blogs who don't have their own websites, or even if you do, to ensure you get a much bigger exposure to what is a global audience of professional people. Therefore by publishing blogs on LinkedIn you automatically have a great opportunity to build and quickly develop your online brand and presence, which for most people is much more difficult to achieve publishing on your own website blog. You need not concern yourself with setting up your own blogsite at this stage. Depending on what you decide to do next, I would think twice about paying to have your own blogsite developed or spending time learning how to do this, as publishing on LinkedIn for many people may well be your best option and it costs nothing other than your time.

Networking

In my experience, some of the biggest fears facing people who are changing careers are:

- Networking – having difficulty explaining your change
- Understanding how to find new opportunities
- Establishing strategies to tap into the 'hidden job market'

Interestingly, most people I come across are already doing some form of networking without realising it, either internally or externally within their organisations almost every day of their employed lives. You may go to conferences and seminars, meet with external suppliers or third party agencies, all of which becomes part of your working life and you take for granted as part of your job. However, when you are proactively networking to help you win through career change, often people see networking differently. Psychologically, networking seems to take on a whole new negative meaning because you are now seeking help to find new career opportunities. Such thinking is yet another limiting belief and perception, because in reality there is little difference as much networking is still just having conversations online or building rapport over a cup of coffee!

What networking is?

Networking is all about making connections and building business relationships which is exactly the same as you would in any employed role. Just as you would share knowledge and information with your networks when employed, you can do the same whilst you're exploring opportunities. Yet again, this is all about changing your mindset.

What networking isn't?

The biggest mistake most people make when starting out on personal networking, to explore opportunities, is the 'give us a job syndrome'. I've seen so many people frighten away potential useful connections because of their overly aggressive approach asking people outright if they have any jobs suitable for them. What should you do? One of the key principles of networking is to view every person you speak to, online or offline, as someone who can introduce you to one or two other contacts who may know someone who can help you or move you one step closer to your desired goal. You should be constantly looking for information and new connections to move forward.

Networking is also a two-way process and **givers gain**. Therefore, one good turn deserves another so always establish how you might be able to help the other person in any networking conversations and communications. Whilst you are networking, listening is often more powerful than talking, whether online or offline. You might think there is no way you could help anybody else, but if you don't ask you will never know. The most successful networkers are always those who think of others first, especially if you become a great connector or freely share useful information. I'm sure you would like to be thought of in this light too, wouldn't you?

Crystallising a need

I've come across many wonderful examples of my clients who have embraced networking in a very targeted and specific way to achieve their career goals. By networking and being introduced, referred or recommended to a potential employer through key and influential contacts, can make a huge difference to your success, especially when looking to make a career change.

It is not always the case that a company has made a decision to recruit an addition to their team. As with many things in life, timing can be all important. As already mentioned in this Chapter, sometimes by being in the right place at the right time you could be the person to crystallise a need they may have been considering but had not formalised.

Below are some wonderful examples of how tapping into different types of networking connections can pay real dividends and crystallise a need.

Please note the same principles are equally as important and apply regardless of whether you are looking for employed roles, setting up your own business, self-employed and looking for any type of contract, project, associate or freelance business opportunities.

Ian's Story

Ian was in the twilight of his career, bored and looking for a new challenge. As with many people, and maybe yourself, Ian could not see the way forward and how to make his change happen. He was applying for jobs in the vague hope of being considered but hadn't really established his true marketability, so even after such a long and varied career, he didn't know who he was and what he had to offer. Ian had inadvertently gone down the 'scattergun' approach and was firing blanks, going nowhere before I started working with him.

Having worked through Steps 2 and 3, it was becoming clearer what was important to Ian in his next career move and why. Essentially, he wanted a final challenge, where he could make a difference and excel within a completely different environment, before moving to the country and into semi-retirement. Ian was blessed with a wide range of excellent skills and talents, a great personality and many other wonderful personal attributes. Unfortunately, like most people, Ian was blissfully unaware of most of these until we started working on Step 3 and his true marketability.

Another key stumbling block was seemingly Ian's reluctance to network. Despite having had many different jobs in completely different business sectors and also being actively involved with a number of sports and community groups, Ian maintained 'he had 'exhausted his networks'. This is something I have heard from a number of people over the years, which is always a smokescreen for 'I am afraid of networking or I don't know how to go about networking to win through my career change!'

Of course Ian hadn't exhausted his contacts at all. When we worked through the 'reverse target model' (to follow shortly) and looked at the different categories, Ian recalled how he had developed a really good relationship with a Director of a supplier in his last job. This was as a result of the Director's exceptional empathy and attention to service detail that allowed him to turn around a major complaint received about a large batch of faulty equipment that Ian had purchased for the company. Having now reluctantly set up his profile on LinkedIn, Ian managed to track down his contact and decided to phone him, as he liked the human contact approach.

What transpired was a real lesson to Ian and anyone reading this book. Why? Because, although his contact was now MD of the company, he remembered Ian and was happy to talk with him, as they clearly had mutual professional respect for each other.

So, having overcome the first barrier, Ian explained how he was looking for a new challenge to see him through the next few years, something he could really get his teeth stuck into and make a difference. The MD asked him to email his CV and said he would think about any contacts he could forward this to who might be looking for someone with his range of skills and business background. Much to Ian's surprise and delight, it appeared at face value that Ian's contact was keen to help him.

Sure enough, a couple of weeks later, Ian got a call from a good contact of the MD he had emailed his CV to. They asked to meet him regarding a potential opportunity. It was all somewhat vague, but the outcome was that the company were expanding and looking to create the position of 'Quality Manager' - a senior position for someone who could set and monitor standards of customer service to maintain operational efficiency. Although Ian had never previously undertaken such a role, the company recognised from the CV and the introduction that he appeared to have the potential skills, attributes and business acumen to be effective in the role. It was now a question of seeing if Ian was a good fit in terms of his personality, general outlook and commitment to the challenge.

There is an amusing but lengthy story that sits behind the sequence of events in the ensuing process, but the outcome was that Ian had crystallised a need and the company created a job especially for him, which was never formally advertised.

I was delighted for Ian, who was very excited but equally bewildered by the unfolding events from the point of making that initial approach to his old supplier contact. When I questioned him about the new job he explained that the role met the majority of his top values and needs and so it was a no brainer. Even more remarkable was that he had been given a blank canvas and his first task was to write his own job description. What a fantastic networking result and way to start a new job and career!

I have shared Ian's story with many people over the years to inspire them to think differently about networking.

When working through my Six Step Career Navigation Cycle to achieve career change, it is only when you shift your mindset and see things from a different perspective, believe in the process and take positive action that you will overcome your fears and limiting beliefs to achieve positive results… just as Ian did!

I have Ian to thank for my 'reverse target networking model'. I developed this because, like Ian, I was finding that many clients (and most people) have a real barrier and limiting beliefs around:

1. Why you should network

2. The positive benefits from networking

3. Understanding what your current network looks like
4. Understanding what networking is and isn't
5. Understanding how to develop and optimise your networks

By using the 'reverse target' approach you will learn how to reframe your thinking around networking as follows:

Key learning points for Networking:

- Networking does not need to be scary
- Networking is a great skill to learn and hone both online and offline
- Networking is not just about you – it is a 2 way process – **givers gain!**
- Focus on gaining recommended contacts and useful information
- Networking helps to identify opportunities
- Networking creates opportunities
- Networking helps you tap into the hidden job market
- Most people genuinely want to help you
- You never know who may unlock the key to your future

Most importantly, don't follow the 'herd'. Instead, bypass the competition and recruitment process (if looking for a different type of job) by networking yourself into situations where you ideally get introduced, referred or recommended, so you are ahead of the game!

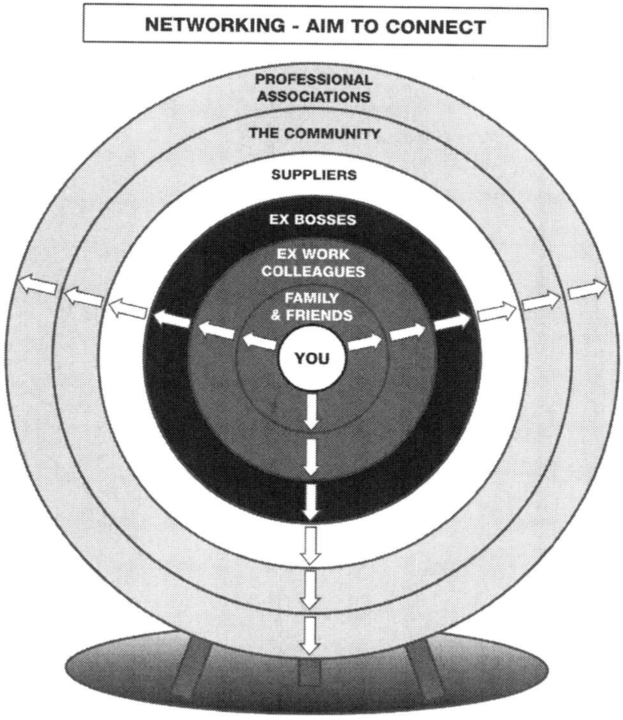

So, how do you go about developing and optimising your networks?

If you are new to networking or you are a reluctant networker, as I was initially during my career transition, the following approach will go a long way to break down your barriers and get you started. Once you get into the swing of networking, you like me and Ian, will never look back and it will become a part of your everyday business life.

The image depicts a simple but highly effective networking approach I developed a number of years ago, which I call the 'reverse target' approach. *Why reverse target?* Because you would normally aim at the bullseye at the middle of the target, wouldn't you? Instead, taking this approach will help you build your networking confidence and ability, because you start within your comfort zone, talking with family and friends. The key is to focus on asking people who they know and who has contacts in the field you are interested in, or who might have knowledge that could steer you in the right direction. As you gain in confidence, you can then work outwards as each category is likely to seem less daunting. The 'Community' can be any contacts in groups or clubs you belong to, e.g. religious, political, hobbies, sports, leisure, your gym etc. Since establishing commonality is one of the most helpful aspects of networking, it should always be easier when you are talking with like-minded people, which you will have seen from the case studies highlighted.

As you gradually move outwards, reaching new targets, you will be gaining new contacts all the time. It is important to understand that it is not just about the initial contacts you make and how you build rapport and relationships with them. You now have an opportunity to develop your networks even further by tapping into other people's contacts as well, which will help you reach a contact currently out of your own circles. This is where networking becomes very powerful and is the principle on which all the Social Media networks such as Facebook and LinkedIn are built, because you never know who it might be possible to connect with and where this might lead you. Remember, you never know who will unlock the key to your future. It will probably be someone you actually don't know right now.

✎ *Exercise – Expanding Your Network*

Following the principles highlighted in the last section, use the example below to create your own spreadsheet or table and highlight people you would ideally like to contact, or definitely need to contact in order to add to your network. Also indicate the best method to contact each person online or offline (i.e. via LinkedIn, Facebook, email or by telephone). You can then prioritise your list and add timescales to ensure you have a target to keep you focused.

Network Category	New Contacts	Method To Connect
Family and friends		
Ex work colleagues		
Ex boss		
Suppliers		
Leisure & community		
Professional associations		

The Hidden Job Market

You may have heard this term before but not understood the importance. The 'hidden job market' is the chunk of the job market which, as it implies, is hidden from the view of most people. What do I mean by 'hidden'? Quite simply - these jobs are not advertised in the public domain, e.g. national press, regional or local press, company websites or recruitment agencies.

What is the size of the hidden Job Market?

I always ask my clients this question to check their knowledge and understanding. What do you think? Most people say around 20% of jobs would not be advertised. If you believe this then you are in for one hell of a shock! Over the last decade, career researchers and commentators have suggested that between 60% to 80% of all jobs are never advertised in the public domain! For management roles, the view is around 80% as the norm. These figures also tend to increase during recession and times of economic uncertainty.

So where are the jobs?

It is often the case that an employer has a need to recruit but due to cost controls has a ban on recruitment advertising. To overcome the inability to advertise, many private sector employers may just source new staff through their own employees. 'Introduce a friend' schemes, where employers pay a fee to the introducing employee once the new recruit has passed any probationary period, are increasingly common.

Why do they do this? Quite simply it is good economics. Existing employees are unlikely to introduce anybody except good candidates because their own reputation is at stake. Employers' 'bounties' can be anything from a couple of hundred pounds to a couple of thousand pounds depending on the sector and the level of the job role. This may seem a lot of money but compared to typical recruitment agency rates, e.g. anything from 10% to 40% of annual salary, this is a massive cost saving.

In a difficult economic climate, many employers are reluctant to use recruitment agencies and executive search companies, except for the most prestigious roles. If we look at a typical middle management role at circa £40,000 per annum, an employer could be paying a recruitment agency an average fee of £8,000 if based on 20% of salary. You can now see why paying existing employees to introduce a friend could be massively cost and time saving to the company.

How do you tap into the hidden Job Market?

In today's rapidly changing marketplace, many job vacancies are only advertised via sector specific groups on LinkedIn, e.g. the largest being HR, Marketing, Finance and IT. If you are not signed up to some of these groups and you are looking for opportunities in these and other sectors, you are very likely to miss out. You have to be 'in it to win it', as I have said before! LinkedIn in general has rapidly become one of the biggest portals for job search and recruitment on the planet! Other key ways to tap into this market are by following the strategies highlighted in this Chapter, e.g. targeted speculative applications, being opportunistic, developing relationships with selected head hunters (who may have exclusivity to recruit) and above all else, effective networking and use of Social Media. I cannot stress enough that you ignore these strategies at your peril!

Portfolio Career Options – How to Work For Passion, Pleasure and Profit!

A Lifestyle Choice

This brings us back to Portfolio Careers. As in my case and for many of my clients, friends and contacts, try forgetting the whole concept of *"A job"* – instead reframe the job concept altogether so that *"It's not about a job or a career necessarily anymore, it's about generating income in a way that meets all your lifestyle objectives"*, which will come from your re-evaluation and income objectives in Chapter 2.

Developing a portfolio career means seeking fulfilment from tapping into your true marketability in terms of your skills, natural talents, attributes, passions and interests. By tapping into your connections, you may open up opportunities for potential collaborations with like-minded people whilst keeping your contacts informed of what you are now offering.

For many people developing a Portfolio Career is also a key lifestyle choice. It is about reshaping your career and redesigning your life. Charles Handy originally coined the term "Portfolio Life" in his book *'The Age of Unreason'* in 1989. He describes a portfolio life as *"a portfolio of activities – some we do for money, some for interest, some for pleasure, some for a cause... the different bits fit together to form a balanced whole... greater than the parts"*.

I remember vividly extolling the virtues of a portfolio career at a career development workshop a number of years ago. One of my delegates leapt out of his chair and punched the air and exclaimed. I wondered what on earth he was doing! Like many people, he had not been able to see past getting another job. However, the realisation that a portfolio career could encompass a mix of voluntary work, self-employed work plus even part-time employed work really excited him. His view was that he would even push trolleys in a supermarket car park a few days a week, if it gave him the flexibility and CHOICE he was looking for. He wanted to develop his business idea, but still needed some income and he wanted to continue his voluntary work one day a week. This was a real 'eureka moment' for him and he was already seeing the possibilities, which was brilliant.

How Can A Portfolio Career Work For You? – Your Opportunity To Reflect

Mindful of Charles Handy's definition above, let's take a closer look at a 'Portfolio Career' and how it can work for ***you***:

"Like the sections of a colourful umbrella, you choose from your selection of strengths, skills and talents to best suit you and your clients. Each segment provides you with an opportunity to challenge, to motivate and to grow. With a firm grip on your umbrella, you hold your portfolio life together and it provides a canopy of choice."

Gail Gibson, 2011

It was Gail's fascinating description of a portfolio career and lifestyle aspect, on a LinkedIn group, that so resonated with me and attracted my attention. It was very apparent there were some real synergies between us by the way we shared similar thinking in the group, so we met. The result was developing our *'How Colourful is Your Umbrella - Creating Your Portfolio of Choice'* Portfolio Career and Lifestyle concept. For a number of years we developed a range of inspirational seminars and Masterclasses and also published a 2 CD/MP3 set audio book.

http://www.stevepreston thecareercatalyst.com/ product/how-colourful-is-your-umbrella-mp3-audio-book/

What we achieved is an excellent example of a mutually beneficial collaboration with a like-minded person, with shared values and beliefs, who has also become a valued and trusted friend. It doesn't get much better than that, does it?

A successful portfolio career and lifestyle is a curious and self-fulfilling mix of challenge, diversity and inspiration. This alternative way of thinking, working and living provides you with an opportunity to embrace choice, freedom and purpose. A portfolio career and life allows you to step aside from conventional, conditioned thinking around the "need to get another job".

Perhaps the greatest aspect of this working lifestyle is that you can choose who you work with, how you work with them, when you work and where you work. You have the flexibility to add and change the strands to 'your colourful umbrella' and for it to transform into '**your** portfolio of CHOICE!'

Gail is reinventing herself again and changing her portfolio, as I write. It is a very exciting time for her and as a great advocate of the portfolio career and creator of the 'colourful umbrella' concept, it has enabled her, like me, to change and add new business and income streams whilst also dropping others where she no longer has the same passion or interest. **This is also so much easier to achieve when you have clarity around what success means to you in your bigger picture life plan.**

I remember many years ago being impressed by an Interim HR Director who worked 4 days a week and on Fridays taught in a school. It was something she loved and it was also a commitment to a close friend. She really valued her teaching job and saw this as a mutually beneficial situation, a key part of her life and around which she planned everything else. We will look more closely at Interim Management in Chapter 5.

Top tip to make your portfolio career work for you

I have never forgotten the best piece of advice I was ever given in relation to portfolio careers, and I will share this with you now.

Find one key strand of work that can pretty much guarantee you regular work, so that this can help cover most of your bills, then develop other business strands alongside this.

I'm sure you will agree, this approach makes perfect sense and also helps to reduce yet another 'fear factor 'or limiting belief that you won't make a portfolio career work.

I now call this developing your 'anchor'. I started using this term as a result of coaching a client who was struggling to see the way forward with her career change until I shared the portfolio career concept with her. She declared excitedly…"I get it. I will find one aspect of regular work that will cover most of my bills, 'my anchor' and I can then then spread my wings and develop other strands of work I love alongside this!" It was by using this wonderful metaphor to see the way forward that she won through her career change!

How will you define your working lifestyle into the future?

What if you were to say, *"I choose to build a working lifestyle based on what I love to do and what I am good at"*. Think about it. You give yourself an opportunity to start a new career path for yourself, one that is built on passion, pleasure and profit.

The concept of the 3 Ps - *"working for passion, pleasure and profit"*, is the way I am now framing portfolio careers, as this clearly resonates with many people. Why? Because, by reframing your career in this way, you give yourself an opportunity to step away from the uncertainty of needing to have a 'traditional job'. By developing a portfolio career you have a golden opportunity to attempt to 'future proof' what you do. Sounds great doesn't it? You have the power to reshape your career and create a more robust framework to allow you to redesign your career and life in the way you want. I will be extolling the virtues of the 3 Ps - "working for passion, pleasure and profit", for my next book, Masterclasses and also when coaching my clients to win through career change.

Here is a simple but poignant *example* of how you might develop a portfolio career based on those important 3 Ps:

Passion:

Think back to the Self Awareness Matrix exercise in Chapter 3, focusing on what attracts, interests and inspires you. These are the magnets in your life e.g. where you have a compelling enthusiasm or desire for activities and work. This could be combining heart, mind and soul.

Pleasure:

The personal reward from doing fulfilling work you love!

Profit:

The financial reward from the different strands of your portfolio. This will vary, depending on the nature of the work you do. However, for many people, each strand is likely to attract a different level of fee paying work. Your ultimate aim is earning enough to provide the working lifestyle you want.

In my case, my portfolio ranges from high fee earning work from coaching executives, to the other end of the spectrum a few pounds or dollars in royalties from this book. I also give my time for free to speak at Business Libraries, Professional

Associations and Job Clubs, which is a way for me to make a contribution and give back into the community. Again, at the other end of the spectrum, I am also well paid as a Keynote motivational speaker at corporate conferences and major career events. Most importantly, it is my CHOICE, as to how I earn a living from my portfolio career, as you can too.

This is a very different concept to focusing on Profit, first and foremost, as many people do. My Amazon best selling ***Portfolio Careers - How to Work for Passion, Pleasure & Profit*** book features many different case studies and nuggets from a mixture of clients and contacts from the UK and around the globe, who I have interviewed. They all agree that if you focus on Profit first, it is unlikely you will be working for your real Passion and extremely unlikely that you will achieve real Pleasure from your job or career.

However, isn't it good to know that can make a living and create a fulfilling working lifestyle by doing work you love? - What could be better than this type of approach?

When I came across this profound quote from Peter Drucker, the renowned business guru, over a decade ago, it really made me sit up and take notice and radically changed my views on work and life:

"Corporations once built to last like pyramids are now more like tents... You can't design your life around a temporary structure."

Harvard Business Review (May1993).

How incredibly perceptive he was and things have only got worse since! The Portfolio Career is an amazing and life changing concept. It is not for everyone but if it sounds enticing, what do you have to lose?

Keep building your momentum

Are you thinking: So many questions, yet not enough answers? Remember the key is to focus on your target. Keep building momentum and tackle everything in manageable chunks. Just as we covered in Chapter 1, the area of mindset is absolutely massive and it is wise to consider this piecemeal. From my experience, the people who tend to make the quickest breakthroughs and fastest transformations are those who are focused, proactive and whose mindset is very strong. If you are determined not to get derailed and can accept that it is in the nature of the career transition and Cycle process that you might move two steps forward and one step back, then providing you have the right attitude, determination and belief in the process and keep following it, you will ultimately succeed.

Mark's Story (continued)

Step 4 – Exploring Opportunities

One Foggy 'Groundhog Day'.

Can you begin to imagine now, just how rewarding this step was for Mark and how it was almost a repeat of his first successful career change?

Yet again I encouraged Mark to talk openly and honestly with his friends about his latest situation at work. As a consequence, his best friend suggested he should apply for a new vacancy in the Information Technology (IT) Support Department where he held the position of Team Leader. Mark just dismissed the idea – "30 years old with no experience in the IT world. You've got to be having a laugh, how could I possibly be a realistic candidate?" The fog began to descend.

However, Mark became intrigued by such an opportunity... and it's good to be so curious and open to possibilities, isn't it? He was bemused to understand how his friend thought he would be capable of changing from a physically demanding career to something so dramatically different.

But what to do next? Here we go again! The challenge was therefore to tackle Mark's mindset, to change his perspective and allow him to appreciate this real opportunity. In the coaching session that followed, I worked with Mark to explore and map out the IT Support role against his values and needs, and to jointly examine the job and person specification in some detail.

This was another fruitful exercise as the new perspective not only enabled Mark to realise that he was able to cover most of job requirements listed but in the person specification, he also discovered the job complemented his personal values. The necessary work ethic, customer service and problem solving skills had all been well developed during his career – he had just not considered working in such a different environment using the same skills set.

It was at this point that Mark began to emerge from the lifting fog and started to realise why his friend had put his reputation on the line in recommending him to his boss. However, there's always that little voice in your head that casts some doubt, isn't there? What if the next job wasn't the right next job and career change? But, what if it was? Did Mark have the courage to press ahead and decide what to do?

...to be continued

- The Person Specification is the most important part of the Job Specification to focus on as this will list the skills, experience and qualifications etc. that the employer sees as being necessary to undertake the role, which you will be assessed against

- Most importantly, many organisations regard these requirements as being 'essential' and/or 'desirable' ... with the latter category providing some leeway when perhaps some skills can be learnt at a later stage

- Never under-estimate or overlook any activities and skills you may have used not just within but also outside the workplace, perhaps in your interests and leisure pursuits

- With some scrutiny and expert help, you may realise that you do actually possess more transferrable skills and personal attributes, which you can readily employ in a different working environment

- As with his previous career change, Mark had the benefit of a great introduction made by a valued and trusted friend who would not have recommended him if he didn't believe he could do the job well

- Often other people, like a coach, will see more of your innate talent than you will yourself

- Introductions, recommendations and referrals are highly likely to give you a competitive advantage and help overcome a lack of experience

Summary

With your jigsaw pieces coming together you can now start developing a laser focus aimed at your future targets.

Here are the key conclusions from Step 4 of the process:

- Be bold - It is never too late to realise aspirations you have always wanted to achieve but never been brave enough or had the time to try
- Follow your passions and you will find a way to make things happen for you
- Don't jump out of the frying pan and into the fire!
- A job is good but it might not be great or the right answer for you, as you do have CHOICE!
- Research and networking are key to exploring and opening up new opportunities
- Set your sights high and step out of your comfort zone to create real opportunities
- Listen to your Inner voice and follow your gut feelings - they are usually right
- You don't have to continue work you don't really enjoy, even if you are good at it
- Be true to yourself and your values and you will be happy
- The Law of Attraction is powerful so focus on your intent and what you want more of
- Now is the time to develop a compelling CV, bios and online profiles
- Learn to love Social Media, especially LinkedIn and develop your online brand and presence to make it work for you
- Take care to manage your online reputation, especially on Facebook

- Keep an open mind - If your *WHY* is strong enough the *WHAT* and *HOW* will follow
- Volunteering or work shadowing are great ways to try something new to see if it's right for you
- Give yourself 'permission' to face your fears head on and banish them, especially about networking!
- Don't let procrastination rule - Find the time and best way for you to work at your career change
- Learn to be opportunistic and you may crystallise a need
- Network your way to tap into the 'hidden job market' and circumnavigate the recruitment process
- A portfolio career, based around the *3 Ps* and working for **Passion**, **Pleasure** and **Profit** into generating the income and lifestyle you want is a whole new world of opportunity and fulfilling option
- It's your future - Don't let other people control it. Take control yourself and learn to become 'the architect of your own future'!
- With the right mindset, belief and positive actions you can achieve almost anything!

Congratulations, you are now ready to move quickly onto **Step 5 - 'Deciding what to do'.**

CHAPTER 5

Deciding What To Do – Step 5

"What we can or cannot do, what we consider possible or impossible is rarely a function of our true capability. It is more likely a function of our beliefs about who we are"

Anthony Robbins

Having started down the path of researching, networking and exploring opportunities, this step of the Cycle is about coming to the right conclusion about what you want to do next. The only thing that can hold you back now is your own fears or limiting beliefs about what is possible. This Chapter also includes practical strategies for taking the next step. It may be that an interest outside work or a previously untapped area of your skills and knowledge has the potential to become a temporary income stream, even form part of a portfolio career or become your new business offering.

Depending on how focused or seriously you have worked on your career change so far, you now need to take full responsibility, in order to decide what to do and achieve a successful outcome. If you have not done so already, start thinking much more clearly about short, medium and longer term goals. You might decide to get an employed job doing something different, as your immediate priority, but know that your ultimate goal is to start your own business or develop a portfolio career. So you may find at this stage that there is a lot of clutter to work through and the array of considerations can grow like 'weeds' that become entangled and can choke your 'new shoots of growth' unless they are tended and the weeds removed. Whatever your current mindset, only **you** can now make things happen to achieve your desired end goal.

The Career 'Trap'

How Did You Choose A Career Or Actually Decide What Work To Do?

You may be reflecting on this question. My experience is that unless you set out with the specific intention of being a doctor, lawyer, nurse, dentist, engineer or other profession and went to university to study for such careers, for the majority of people it was more about luck, chance, peer pressure, parental and teacher influences or just falling into jobs. My thoughts are substantiated by numerous conversations with clients, friends, associates, connections and discussions in online forums.

As a result, you don't necessarily have a career plan but develop your career by working for a specific company for a while, get promoted and grow your career within that company. You then move on, doing similar work in another company and before you know where you are you have unwittingly entered the 'Career Trap' and become ensnared. What tends to happen for many people is that they just roll on in the same old way following a linear career path. Suddenly, they reach the point of no return because they are fed up and want to change or the rug is pulled from under them, in which case they are forced to take action. I'm sure this sounds like a familiar story.

The CHOICE Now Is To Do Something Different And Reinvent Yourself

For those of you who've had long careers, you will find there are so many more opportunities to change into new and different careers than when you first set out. With the advent and phenomenal growth of the Internet, there are now multitudes of different ways to earn a living, which would have previously been inconceivable. We will look at a range of possible options in this Chapter. The difference now, is you do have the CHOICE and the chance to plan and become the architect of your own future to create the work and lifestyle you want.

It is my experience at this stage of the Career Navigation Cycle process that you will now either be flying and ready to make key decisions about what you wish to do next, or you might still be confused and need to untangle some weeds in your mind. What do I mean by this? Consider carefully what is stopping you from making the decision about what to do next? Having provided you with all the strategies you need to explore opportunities in Chapter 4, realistically, the only thing that can be holding you back is you.

If so, ask yourself:

- Are you still unsure whether you wish to be employed or self-employed?
- Do you doubt your ability to run your own business?
- Are you still unclear on what it is you can do next?
- Do you doubt your ability to make a successful career change?

Some of your answers may still be limiting beliefs which you need to challenge. Read on and see where this leads you.

PIT STOP

WINNING STEER

Bear in mind that at this step of the Cycle you are likely to journey back and forth to step 4 and maybe even Steps 2 and 3 in order to clarify your thinking. You should not view this as negative or that you are not making progress. Accept it as a natural part of your journey and the career change process, as you narrow down your thinking and make key decisions about what to do next.

Moving From Chaos To Clarity

Untangle The Weeds In Your Mind

A garden entangled and enmeshed with weeds can only give rise to 'chaos' and yet some simple tidying will allow you to see the path and gain 'clarity'. Likewise, at this stage of the Cycle, as you move through your voyage of self-discovery to reach your next destination, it is important to do a spot of metaphorical gardening and some 'weeding of the mind'.

The acronyms below demonstrate the typical emotions and feelings experienced during this journey **from CHAOS to CLARITY.** How many of these resonate with you?

FROM CHAOS COMES CLARITY

C = Confusion
H = Helplessness
A = Anger
O = Obstacles
S = Scattergun

C = Courage
L = Lucidity
A = Awareness
R = Revelation
I = Intent
T = Transparency
Y = Yearning

If you're still struggling to find the lucidity, your revelation and your intent is not yet transparent, you will almost certainly find the answers by rereading some of the earlier Chapters and reviewing the work you have done from the many exercises in the book. I guarantee the answers will either be staring you in the face or they are hidden because you may still have some limiting beliefs to overcome first. Don't forget, you are more than likely still on an emotional roller coaster and you may have some twists and turns to maneuver before you head on the upswing towards your new career and life path.

The Thief Of Time

"Time is what we want most, but what we use worst."

William Penn, Founder of the Province of Pennsylvania, USA, 1644 -1718

This poignant quote became so reminiscent of my own situation during my transition, when I often felt time was both a blessing and a curse. I now realise that timescales for such a career change journey will vary depending upon your personal circumstances. For instance, if you are returning to work, following a career break, then you are likely to have far more time to work at your career change than someone who still has a full on day job.

Some say that procrastination is the thief of time, but I now say this needs to be balanced with a degree of patience and planning.

As I've stated from the outset, you are on a journey and there is no set time to make your career change. Everyone will have different motivations and timescales with six months to a year being very typical. What often happens is that you start off down the road thinking you will get another job doing something completely different and as time goes by, as part of your ongoing re-evaluation, the more work you do on yourself and the more self-aware you become, you start to think:

- Maybe there are other options after all?

- You don't really want to work for anyone else anymore
- You have had it applying for lots of jobs without success
- Maybe you can set up a business of your own?

Remember *Ben Sweetland's quote "Success is a journey not a destination".*

Now Is The Time To Get Serious!

From my experience, unless you have the benefit of working through a process, such as my Cycle, to get you to the point of clarity, you can easily be derailed. Before you know it, six months can easily pass and what have you got to show for it? It is at this point where I often get potential new clients contacting me, as they are frustrated at their lack of progress.

Building momentum is key to achieving a successful career change. As I have mentioned repeatedly, there is no one size fits all magic wand or Holy Grail. However, I can guarantee that by following my Six Step Cycle process, believing in the process and taking positive action, that you will ultimately achieve a successful career change. If you are not making the progress you expected then you need to review what is holding you back. Invariably, what is likely to be holding you back is one of these factors:

- Lack of motivation
- Procrastination
- Afraid to get out of your comfort zone

Regardless of your situation, at this Step in the Cycle, now is an excellent time to review, take stock and refocus. If you haven't done so already, now is the time to start some serious action planning, which we will look at in Chapter 6.

Time To Step Out Of Your Comfort Zone

Sometimes, at this stage of the Cycle you can lose focus and may get distracted. Alternatively, you might be raring to go in order to determine what you want to do next. This can be both exciting and scary. Procrastination is the killer for a huge percentage of people during the career transition process. I can certainly put up my hand and honestly say that was the case with me. Deciding what to do for a lot of people is scary because, having completed your research and explored opportunities, the realisation could be that your passions, interests, true marketability and values are all providing evidence for you, which now needs decisions. However, only you can take the responsibility for your success and make anything happen. For some people this will take you well outside your comfort zone but for others, it will become the 'thrill of the chase'!

One of the most important things I've learnt, as a career and personal development expert, is that you don't achieve anything worthwhile in your life without coming out of your comfort zone. As long as you understand this, are prepared to work at it, then you will get the ultimate reward of finding a job, career or work you love, so you can lead a fulfilling life. We will revisit stretching out of your comfort zone in more detail in Chapter 6.

Take Time To Get Any Additional Support You May Need

If you really are stuck at this point, especially if you are now lacking motivation, stuck in procrastination mode or frightened to leave your comfort zone, it will definitely pay you to get additional support. This might be a Career Coach, Mentor or Adviser who can add real value to help you turn your ideas into reality or in the case of a Career Coach, help you come up with ideas in the first place. What support you need depends on what your decisions are at this stage.

You may feel that you would benefit from bringing this book to life by allowing me to coach and guide you through the Six Steps of my Cycle. If so, then my innovative and inspirational online programme containing inter-active video and audio content will be just right for you: *'Navigate Your Way To A Brighter Future – Six steps to transform your career and life'* Online Career Change and Transition Programme. This popular programme is proven to work particularly well when used in conjunction with this book.

You may decide to set up a specific type of business and would feel more confident working with someone who has already done so successfully. If so, your best bet would be to find a suitable mentor. A good example, is a client I was working with a few years ago, who was recommended to me because he wanted to break free from the shackles of The National Health Service and explore a career change:

Malcolm's Story

Malcolm wanted to understand how he could use his undoubted skills, attributes and passions to do something different that would be of interest to him in the latter stages of his career and provide him with a sense of purpose and fulfilment. I coached him through a few sessions round the Cycle to Step 4, where one option he was considering was setting up his own consultancy to do work in the Health Service and Charity sectors. At this point, I networked him to a contact of mine who had already trodden this same path. Whereas, I would have continued to coach him to reach definite conclusions, by taking this approach he had the benefit of an industry specialist who was able to share her knowledge and experience and act as a mentor for Malcolm. Having such a valued and trusted mentor gave him a head start and was also a great boost to his confidence, to follow a similar path.

Before you engage any additional support, just as you would with a builder or electrician etc., make sure the person you choose comes highly recommended. This is a key investment of your time and money, so it is important you have the right chemistry with your coach, mentor or adviser.

Unfortunately there are plenty of people who will take your money without a thought, so always check for valid testimonials plus accreditations from relevant professional associations, e.g. Association for Coaching or Institute of Leadership and Management.

The Universal Laws Of Success And Achievement

Why Are Some People More Successful Than Others?

I have made various mentions of Brian Tracy in the earlier Chapters of the book. A remarkable psychologist, author and speaker, he has dedicated much of his life to studying Universal Laws of Success and Achievement, some dating back to Aristotle. These revelations can be life changing for you, too, as success is not a miracle, an accident nor is it a matter of luck. There are many universal laws which affect success, and understanding these laws puts a completely different perspective on life. Let's now consider three such laws:

(i)The Law of Cause and Effect: Everything happens for a reason; for every effect there is a specific cause

Aristotle asserted that we live in a world governed by law, not chance. He stated that everything happens for a reason, whether or not we know what it is. He said that every effect has a specific cause or causes. Every cause or action has an effect of some kind or another, whether we can see it and whether we like it or not. This law says that achievement, wealth, happiness, prosperity and business success are all the direct and indirect effects or results of specific causes or actions. This simply means that, if you can be clear about the effect or result you want, you can probably achieve it. Also, by studying others who have achieved the same goal to which you aspire, e.g. starting up your own business or achieving financial independence, **by replicating the actions they took, you in turn can achieve the same results.** This law is the very is the principle that my *'Toolkit for Life'* (Chapter 1) is based on. When you change your thinking (cause) and work through the *'Toolkit'* you ultimately change your results and life, which are very definite effects!

(ii) The Law of Attraction

You are a living magnet; you invariably attract into your life the people, situations and circumstances that are in harmony with your dominant thoughts. The Law of Attraction states that our thinking creates and brings to us whatever we think about. In essence this means that like attracts like and that by focusing on positive or negative thoughts, one can bring about positive or negative results.

This is the emphasis of The Law of Attraction, which we first started exploring in Chapter 1 and we revisited in Chapter 4, where we explored the importance of focusing on what you want and your intent. In Chapter 1, I explained the importance of your mindset. At this stage of the Cycle and career change process, having a positive mindset becomes ever more important. For instance:

(a) If your thinking has always been and still is *"I can't see myself in a new career and I know I'm going to be in the same position in 6 months' time"*, then this is exactly what is likely to manifest, as you are focusing your energy on what you don't want.

(b) Conversely, if your focus and thinking is and has been *"I will have made my career change within six months into a new career and work I love"*, then this is more than likely what will happen.

Isn't it good to see the difference in these two statements and the switch to focusing on what you do want with positive energy? By taking this approach you will take control of your career to become the architect of your own future in the timescale that works for you.

(iii) The Law of Requisite Variety

I discovered the Law of Requisite Variety when working with one of my clients, who is now an NLP (Neuro Linguistic Programming) Master Practitioner. This law is taken from the field of cybernetics and essentially states that the person with the greatest flexibility of behaviour will control the system. If what you're doing isn't working then by doing 'something else' has much more chance of success, as there are always alternatives. In these circumstances you can carry on doing the same old things and continue to produce unwanted results, or you can adapt your behaviour as necessary until you get your desired outcome. This might be considered 'common sense', so you don't want to be one of these people trying to beat their head against a brick wall, do you?

Your Career Options

The world of work has changed dramatically over the past few decades. The Internet and new technology have transformed the way we work. 'Digital nomads' are springing up all around the globe and proving that you can make a living working remotely anywhere with good mobile technology and most importantly WIFI.

If you've had a long career in one sector, it is highly likely you will be oblivious to the wealth of new career and work options now available. In today's online, digital 24/7 environment of the 'information and knowledge worker', pretty much anything is possible, regardless of your age. You certainly won't be short of options, which in itself can be both exciting and scary. Either way, I'm sure you will agree this is great cause for encouragement, as you certainly do have CHOICE!

I have challenged you throughout this book to consider whether you wish to be employed or self-employed or maybe even develop a portfolio career. However, there are still multiple opportunities within self-employed and portfolio career options. Before you come to any definite conclusions, let's now look at a range of options which you may have never previously considered, including some web and home based businesses. **This is just a small sample, so to find out more, you will need to continue with your research, just as in Step 4.** Opportunities to earn money from the web are far too numerous to mention. However, I have highlighted a couple of interesting examples which involve little or no investment, minimal training and are becoming increasingly popular due to the quick turnaround time to be able to trade.

Consulting

What is consulting?

Consulting is becoming an increasingly broader industry, incorporating roles such as management consultants, IT consultants, recruitment consultants, business advisers, training consultants, HR consultants, marketing consultants, social media and digital media consultants to name just a few. Whichever way you look at it consultancy is a varied profession, with projects and clients changing constantly. This can be the beauty but also the challenge of this profession.

Definition of consulting

"The provision to businesses of objective advice and assistance relating to the strategy, structure, management and operations of an organisation in pursuit of its long term purposes and objectives. Such assistance may include the identification of options with recommendations; the provision of additional resources; and/or the implementation of solutions."

The Institute of Consulting

In a nutshell, a consultant provides external advice for organisations that require specialist expertise or an objective outside perspective on their business. For many professionals, if you are an expert in your field, consulting is an obvious, reasonably 'safe' sensible option, just as it was with me when I started my own business.

What makes a successful consultant?

- You are well respected for your knowledge and expertise in your sector
- You always work to high professional standards

- You have developed a good network with many valued and trusted connections
- You are a strategic thinker good at seeing the bigger picture
- You have excellent communication skills with the ability to highlight key information either in written reports or verbally, to enable stakeholders or key decision makers to take action
- You are able to work well at all levels of the organisation, especially with senior executives and the Board
- You have a strong personal brand and project an air of confidence and self-belief
- If you don't know the answer you know someone who does and can collaborate with them to achieve your desired goal
- You can sell and market yourself effectively
- You can use previous projects to highlight your competency whilst being mindful of confidentiality

Does this sound like you? If so, consulting could be an option. If consulting sounds appealing but you have some key gaps to fill, you can explore opportunities for developing what skills you feel are missing.

Interim Management

Interim Management is becoming increasingly important in the business mix, being a much more hands on alternative to Management Consultancy. Providing the temporary provision of management resources and skills, Interim Management can be seen as the short term assignment to manage a period of transition, crisis or change within an organisation.

In this situation, a permanent candidate may be unnecessary or impossible to find at short notice as there may be a skills or availability shortage within the organisation.

It is estimated that the Interim Management industry is worth approximately a billion pounds a year in the United Kingdom – that is big business by anyone's standards. Across all sectors, tens of thousands of interims are employed to cover unexpected gaps, deliver key projects, or drive change and growth. Interims are seen as a source of competitive advantage which is the best description of the way they are used in today's market.

Sought after interims are:

- Experienced independent executives or project managers
- Experts in their field with specialist skills
- High level performers with gravitas and a proven track record of delivery and achievement
- Engaged by businesses on a project basis to solve problems
- Required to hit the ground running and deliver results quickly before moving on to the next assignment
- Perceptive, tenacious, flexible and adaptable to new environments
- Strong communicators with excellent interpersonal and people management skills
- Able to see the bigger picture while maintaining a hands on operational focus
- Able to readily engage stakeholders
- Able to operate autonomously or as a part of a team as required

Which Report utility provider, is another increasingly popular example of a well-respected MLM organisation.

Joining a MLM company has a low cost of entry, especially as they usually provide all the training and support you will need to get started and become successful. You are "signing up" to represent that company's product and services and business opportunities. You can share the rewards from this system of business operation if you're willing to put in the hard work at the beginning. Once you've created a critical mass of sales, fed by a combination of your own personal sales and income generated by your down line team, then you should expect to see your total income really take off. MLM has made many millionaires but it is not for everyone. The work you have done in Step 2 around your Values and Needs plus Step 3 around your *true marketability* will help you determine whether MLM is something you may wish to pursue.

Franchises

Buying a franchise gives your commercial plans a head start by adopting an already successful business model. There's a lot to be said for opting for the franchise route, but as with everything you need to thoroughly research any opportunity, because a franchisor is the business rights owner of the operation concept. A franchisee is someone who buys the license rights from the franchisor to operate the business in a particular location for an agreed period of time. A financial investment gives you a readymade business package.

Business format franchising – where full training is provided, together with use of trademarks and a complete system of doing business to include hiring and training staff, site selection, shop fitting and design plus advertising and marketing support. McDonald's, Burger King, Subway and Domino's Pizza are examples of business format franchising. Be aware that a substantial financial investment is required to

- Looking for Interim Management as a career choice rather than a stepping stone to the next permanent job

Common characteristics of interims

Across all sectors and nearly all functions, successful interims tend to demonstrate one characteristic in common: they are able to swiftly engage diverse groups of stakeholders. That ability is so important in an interim assignment, since interims need to hit the ground running, very often executing projects or implementing initiatives that span a number of organisational departments, as well as internal and external stakeholders at all levels.

Interim assignments at the senior level often also require the capability to coach and mentor, since you are there to leave a legacy of value by transferring knowledge, rather than creating a culture of dependency (which has earned management consultancy a bad name in recent times). Even without the reforms and financial challenges, many organisations value the "task and finish" approach that interim managers bring to a project. The interim manager's career depends on each assignment resulting in an excellent outcome. It is also true that interim managers can be objective and speak hard truths, often helping new solutions to emerge, without worrying about their job prospects within the organisation.

Interim Management is difficult to get into but once you develop a reputation you can be in constant demand and make a great living. Interim Management might also be an option to sit within a portfolio career. Does this sound like you? If so Interim Management could be an option.

What is the difference between an interim and a temp or contractor?

An important distinction to make is the difference between the temp/contract market and genuine interim roles. While temporary roles are typically tactical (maintaining steady state), interim roles require genuine change agents who can demonstrate knowledge transfer, legacy creation, and a consistently compelling return on investment.

Some people look at the interim route for the lifestyle benefits of not having a permanent role. I know of a number of interims, including some of my clients, who work on highly paid projects for a few months then take time out to travel or for other lifestyle projects, before seeking their next interim role. Equally, for others the reality can be very different. At senior level, interims tend to agree that they are pursuing a vocational call; the challenge of short term, high pressure assignments that place responsibility and accountability squarely on their shoulders. For many, the challenge and excitement of moving between organisations, even sectors or countries is far more of a draw than any perceived flexibility. As always, you do have CHOICE!

Coaching And Mentoring

Both coaching and mentoring are processes that enable both individual and business clients to achieve their full potential. Although similar, there are fundamental differences and views vary widely as to their exact nature. The following definitions have served me as the basis for training many managers over the years to embrace coaching and mentoring.

(i) Mentoring

What is mentoring?

- Derived from Greek mythology - Odysseus, King of Ithaca, went to fight the Trojan War and entrusted his son Telemachus to the care and direction of his entrusted friend, Mentor
- 'Mentor' is now synonymous with trusted adviser, friend, teacher, wise person

- Oxford dictionary definition 'experienced and trusted adviser'

How does mentoring work?

Mentoring enables an individual (mentee) to work with and follow in the path of an 'older and wiser' colleague who is the Confidante, Teacher, Role Model, Adviser, Friend, Helper who can pass on knowledge, experience and open doors to otherwise out of reach opportunities. I was Mentor to a number of people in my management career and you may also have mentored various subordinates to help them develop their careers. Or you may have developed an area of specialism which you could demonstrate as an expert and mentor newcomers.

External mentors are only different in the fact that they are independent of the organisation; therefore have no line responsibility for the 'mentee'. External mentors are being heavily used in a number of different ways to support businesses e.g.:

- Business start-up
- Business growth
- Young entrepreneurs
- Specific individual progression within organisations (especially senior executives) where they do not have the internal resource

There are a number of government initiatives, charities and social enterprises which have funding for mentoring schemes to support a range of people. They are constantly looking for skilled professionals to train with them, often to achieve accreditations. Such roles are often, but not always, voluntary rather than self-employed fee paying roles. However, as with other work experience, they can be an excellent way for you to gain credibility as an external mentor to benefit you in the longer term.

(ii) Coaching

What is Coaching?

Coaching gained massively in popularity in the nineties and into the new millennium, as individuals and businesses started to realise the transformational value that the coaching approach can bring. This is especially true at key times of change to enable people or businesses to move from where they are now to where they want to be. This is what excites me about coaching. There are a million and one definitions of coaching, here is mine: *"Coaching is facilitating the process of unlocking potential to achieve specific personal or business goals."* There are many more complex definitions. However, this works for me as it is simple and I hope you agree, self-explanatory.

Essentially, Coaching is a form of personal development. It is the process by which individuals are enabled, through questioning and discussion to achieve specific goals, e.g. to change careers, to solve problems. Or they may wish to transfer their learning to the workplace, in order to improve their personal performance, gain insights about themselves, their capabilities and potential.

How does coaching work?

- Developing an individual's performance by unlocking their capabilities through guided questioning, the use of coaching tools and conversation
- Supporting the coachee as a facilitator, helping to raise their awareness through analysis and reflection
- Facilitating the coachee to arrive at their own ideas and solutions

- A good coach should be able to develop a powerful relationship with the coachee based on honest and nonjudgmental dialogue
- Challenging perceptions and behaviour in a way that will enable the coachee to make significant transformations or performance improvements
- Because coaching involves the participation of the coachee to find their own solutions and agree the actions they will take, it drives deeper and more lasting behavioural change than other forms of training

In general, although there will be exceptions, coaching should not be directional, as the coach does not provide answers to specific problems. Instead they will facilitate the process of self resolution through specific questioning. Therefore the coach does not need to be an expert in the specific area requiring development but highly skilled in questioning and active listening. However, there inevitably comes a point in the coaching relationship when the coachee will ask the coach for very specific advice or recommendations. When thinking about developing a coaching practice, it pays you to become an expert in a specific niche so you can add even more credibility and value to the coaching relationship.

There are numerous forms of speciality or niche coaching. To help me get my first book project off the ground, I worked with Leda Sammarco, a 'writer's coach'. Leda was recommended to me as someone who could help me put structure around my book idea and turn it into reality.

I owe Leda a huge debt, as although I have written dozens of articles, writing a book is a different ball game. I would not have engaged Leda if I did not know she was a specialist in her field, as I had many questions and much to learn!

Sports coaching tends to be much more directional, although a good coach will often question the coachee about why something is either working well or not, before giving their view. This is a much more powerful approach, as the coachee will often give reasons and thoughts that the coach may not have considered. The coach might only be looking at things from a technical perspective, rather than physical or psychological.

Other examples of coaching:

- Life Coaching
- Executive Coaching
- Performance Coaching
- Corporate/Business Coaching
- Small Business Coaching
- Group/Team Coaching
- Relationship Coaching
- Parent Coaching
- Retirement Coaching
- Youth Coaching

In my niche as a Career Coach, I specialise in redundancy support (outplacement) and career change mainly for professionals and executives. Although I work with all levels of people, I made the decision to focus on these aspects and client groups as I enjoy them the most. It also makes it easier for me to market my services rather than trying to be all things to all people.

Other forms of coaching will also have their 'micro niches', e.g. Relationship Coaching. I know a number of coaches who specialise in Divorce Coaching. This is a sad statement in itself but clearly there is a need and they are making a good living in this particular niche. I mentioned my associate Debbie Smith, a Personal Branding and Impact Coach, in Chapter 3. Although Debbie works with many clients, she has targeted female executives and professionals. The reasons: firstly because of her affinity with this group but also because there is a real need. There is a widely held view that female professionals struggle with issues around confidence, self-belief and image. As a result they can often fail to create the impact required to compete with male counterparts, losing out on key jobs or not achieving their true financial worth. Coaching is a great way to overcome this.

If you wish to become a coach, I suggest you develop a niche that taps into your personal values, needs, interests and passions. You can then build your knowledge base and learn any new skills required, although your true niche may take time to evolve. It will also pay you to gain a professional coaching qualification, as it is becoming increasingly difficult to get work without one. Coaching has become a very crowded and competitive market. By finding your right niche and having the right qualifications you will have a much greater chance of success.

Associate Work

Instead of being totally reliant on marketing yourself or your business, another option is for you to work for an established business, which uses a team of associates in your field of specialism, e.g. Training. This is exactly what my company does. As my company has grown over the years, I have continually added to my associate team for specialist projects, e.g. Outplacement, Executive, Management and Team Coaching and Development.

When I started out as self-employed, in addition to marketing and delivering projects for my own business,

I was an associate for a training company and have also been an associate for a few HR and Career Management Consultancies. The benefits are that you do not have to look for the business but the downside is that you are unlikely to be able to negotiate your fees, as these will usually be set by the company. Being an associate is also a good option as part of a portfolio career.

WINNING STEER

As an associate, you will need to work under the guidelines of the company engaging you. This usually means working under their brand rather than yours. Some companies insist you sign an associate agreement before you undertake any work. If so, be especially mindful of any clauses which may affect the ownership and use of your own intellectual property.

Virtual Assistants

If you have previously held a highly responsible secretarial, PA or administrative role, have excellent PC and organisational skills and are looking for the flexibility to work from home around your family commitments, this could be an ideal option for you. A virtual assistant (typically abbreviated to VA) is typically self-employed (although some might be employed by a large VA company) and provides remote professional administrative, technical, creative or social media assistance to small businesses on an hourly, project specific or ongoing basis. With modern technology it is possible for a skilled VA to perform a range of key tasks, adding real value to a number of different small businesses, rather than just working for one company. I know many VA's who have interesting portfolio careers with their VA work being their 'anchor' and main income strand combined with other home based activities to achieve their income and lifestyle requirements.

With new communication tools and transmission technologies, it is now possible to have a Virtual Assistant who can answer your phone remotely without the caller's knowledge. This is an excellent way for small businesses to add a personal touch in the form of a receptionist without the additional cost of hiring someone, whilst also providing 24/7 coverage.

I engaged the services of a recommended VA to transcribe my first two audio books. This proved invaluable and a huge time saver. Also, rather unexpectedly, they recommended my products to others, which was an added bonus. I would definitely use them again for other specialist admin support on a project basis, as they are experts in such work and I am not!

E-Lancing

This is a massively growing trend for freelancers to undertake work, usually remotely, which is commissioned by self-employed professionals and small businesses through e-lancing websites, e.g. Freelancer.com and Fiverr.com These sites provide a huge portal for businesses to post projects online for freelancers to then battle it out pitching their skills and rates to win the work. It is rapidly becoming an option for people looking at novel ways to generate an ad hoc income, often as part of a portfolio career and lifestyle approach. It's also great for companies looking for low cost alternatives to fixed staff overheads. In demand professionals range from app developers, graphic designers, web developers to translators, transcribers and voice over artists.

Although e-lancing does offer another useful option to generate income, your competition will be global, including many skilled counterparts in third world and upcoming economies, who are fast becoming masters of marketing themselves at ultracompetitive rates.

WINNING STEER

As with any business opportunity, you must do your homework first and research thoroughly to determine if this cut throat marketplace is right for you. You don't want to spend precious time pitching for work at rates you cannot afford, as this will be counterproductive, won't it?

Web Based Businesses

The internet has created a whole new generation of millionaires, and quite a few billionaires, since its inception. Globalisation suddenly had a whole new vehicle to make it real and entrepreneurs had a completely new route to market. What are now iconic global brands such as Amazon, eBay and Google sprang up from nowhere in no time at all. However, the internet has also enabled any entrepreneur with a website to trade online and build a business from a home PC, laptop or computer tablet etc.

Starting an online business can be as simple as setting up a basic shop on eBay to sell a few wholesale items, to coming up with a completely new online concept with a novel way of monetising it. The beauty of the online business is that it can work for just about anyone. You don't need a fancy degree or to be based in any particular location to succeed. You can also start off small, work on your business part-time or even view it as a hobby before you decide whether to commit to it. You could turn a hobby into a business or sell products by mail order or provide a service directly to customers online. The key criteria:

- You are opportunistic
- Reasonably IT savvy or if not, you have somebody specialist working on your behalf
- You have good business acumen

Looking at these criteria, maybe running a web based business now sounds appealing and something you could seriously consider?

Forex Trading (Foreign Exchange)

Although forex is the largest financial market in the world, it is relatively unfamiliar territory for small traders. Forex was primarily the domain of large financial institutions, multinational corporations and secretive hedge funds. How times have changed with the explosion of the internet. With minimal training you can quickly start trading as an individual investor. The majority of people I know who do trade, have made it part of a portfolio career to supplement income from other sources. And of course, there are some people for whom it is their primary source of income.

What is the Forex Market used for?

The Forex market is a global decentralised financial market for the exchange of currencies. Forex trading involves transactions in which one party purchases a quantity of one currency by paying in a quantity of another currency. Around the world various financial centres act as hubs for trading between a wide range of different types of buyers and sellers, 24 hours a day except weekends. It is the foreign exchange market that determines the value of one country's currency relative to another's, e.g. UK pound vs. the US dollar. The Forex market also provides a medium for speculation which works to add deeper liquidity into the market, making exchange rates less volatile. The "carry-trade" is facilitated via the Forex market. This is a trade in which investors can buy high yielding currencies against low yielding currencies and profit from the higher yielding interest rate.

I know people who 'play' the Forex market. Although you can stand to make substantial gains, similar to stocks and shares, you are in effect 'gambling' on the currency market and should be aware of the risks. As with any trading, markets can fluctuate and become volatile as a result of circumstances totally outside of your control - so exercise some caution.

Product Creation – Developing Information Products

Have you ever thought it would be great to earn income from a passion, interest or knowledge you have by sharing it with others, regardless of whether you're physically working? How cool would it be to earn income while you are sleeping, on holiday enjoying yourself or when you aren't well enough to work, whilst also making a difference to the lives of other people? There are a number of ways to generate passive income, i.e. rather than swapping time for money, you earn income from information products you have created using your expertise e.g.:

- Audio books
- Downloadable MP3s or other high perceived value digitally downloadable products
- Paid for pre-recorded webinars and teleseminars
- Online and home study programmes
- Books and E books
- DVD or CD recordings from seminars and workshops
- Monthly subscriptions to membership sites

In today's world of instant access to information and knowledge, being able to create high quality products, at surprisingly low cost, can open up a whole new world of lucrative income opportunities.

What do you need to produce information products?

- A website set up to sell online products with an integrated shopping cart
- A passion, interest, or other knowledge and expertise to share with others
- Technology to produce and edit your product, e.g. webinar or audio book
- A strong social media presence, e.g. Facebook, Twitter and LinkedIn
- Marketing support or understanding of how to get your product to market

I still marvel and get the same thrill today when I receive emails on holiday telling me someone has just purchased one of my audio books or online programmes, while I am enjoying myself! Like most modern technology, this is becoming cheaper to buy and easier to use by the day. You can find someone you know, or through your networks, to outsource the technical stuff, as I do and you only focus on being the information resource. Whatever approach you take, you put in the hard work up front to develop your product and can then reap the rewards afterwards, time and again! So, what knowledge and expertise do you have that you could turn into information products? Lots I'm sure.

Affiliate Schemes

Simply put, affiliate programmes, also called **associate programmes**, are arrangements in which an online merchant website pays affiliate websites a commission to send them traffic or sell their products. These affiliate websites post links to the merchant site and are paid according to a particular agreement. This agreement is usually based on the number of people the affiliate sends to the merchant's site, or the number of people they send who buy something or perform some other action. Some arrangements pay according to the number of people who visit the page containing their merchant site's banner advertisement.

Basically, if a link on an affiliate site brings the merchant site traffic or money, the merchant site pays the affiliate site according to their agreement. Recruiting affiliates is an excellent way to sell products online, but it can also be a cheap and effective marketing strategy; it's a good way to get the word out about your site.

There are at least three parties in an affiliate programme transaction:

- The customer
- The affiliate site
- The merchant site

In 1996, Jeff Bezos, CEO and founder of Amazon.com, popularised this idea as an Internet marketing strategy. Amazon.com attracts affiliates to post links to individual books for sale on Amazon.com, or for Amazon.com in general, by promising them a percentage of the profits if someone clicks on the link and then purchases books or other items. The affiliate helps make the sale, but Amazon. com does everything else. They take the order, collect the money and ship the book to the customer. With over 500,000 affiliate Web sites now participating, Amazon. com's programme is a resounding success.

Over the past few years, affiliate programmes have grown enormously in popularity, taking many interesting forms. For many websites that don't deal much in e-commerce (selling products or services online) themselves, functioning as an affiliate is a good way to participate in e-commerce. This could be another simple way for you to earn passive income, i.e. not swapping time for money but by riding on the back of other companies' need to sell products by expanding their distribution networks. Equally, for someone like me, who has a range of online products, this is a way for me to get much wider exposure by finding affiliates to market my products.

Multi-Level Marketing

Multi-Level Marketing, or MLM, is a system for selling goods or services through a network of distributors. Multi-level marketing, also called network marketing, is a flexible way to create a second part-time income stream that has the potential to develop into a full-time business occupation. People who join multi-level marketing sales operations do so self-employed and therefore are responsible for managing their own tax matters. After paying a joining fee and completing the training period, new members become known as independent distributors. Remuneration is directly related to their sales performance and the performance of people who join their sales team. The whole concept of multi-level marketing depends upon word of mouth with distributors selling to individuals who subsequently join the sales effort by becoming members of the team.

MLM – A marketing system that's stood the test of time

The most successful MLM companies have been established for a number of years and have developed their product range, business organisation and training programmes to maximise returns. Tupperware have been holding their famous parties for over 60 years. Avon cosmetics have been established over 50 years; Herbalife and Forever Living have been trading for over 30 years. In the UK, Utility Warehouse, the top rated

take on a major high street name like McDonald's and Burger King. To open a McDonald's restaurant can cost anything from £125,000. A franchisee will also be expected to have a healthy financial reserve for working capital.

Products and trade name franchising – the key contribution here is the product or service to be sold. The franchisee takes on the identity and branding and acts as an official representative of the parent company. Trademarks and logos are provided, as well as advertising, sales and marketing support. The business investor buys the products from the brand name company under the franchise law and sells them to interested parties. This type of operation is well established in the automotive and soft drinks markets.

There are multitudes of franchise opportunities available in almost every business discipline, including accountancy firms, office cleaning companies, HR consultancies, travel agencies etc. If franchising appeals, explore franchise opportunities that:

- Appeal to you and to your personality
- Are in high demand
- Have little or no direct competition in your local area
- Nationally, or even internationally known brand with proven consumer / trade demand
- Clear and unambiguous license terms to define franchise territory and agreement period
- Access to signage (if relevant) plus sales and marketing support
- Full initial training – for brand, product and business operation
- Access to ongoing training – and any free, or payment terms of, future training

- Back office business support systems
- Details of the financial status and track record of franchisor
- Provide evidence of a profitable business model

The principle is simple - some companies choose to grow, not by developing in the conventional way, but by granting a license to others to sell their product or service. There are clear advantages to this.

As the voice and self-regulating body of the franchising industry in the UK, the British Franchise Association (BFA), is well placed to educate individuals and businesses about the opportunities that franchising, as a successful business model, can bring. The BFA offers a number of franchise seminars at a range of locations across the UK.

Buying Into An Existing Business In Part Or Whole

If you are in the fortunate position of being in a strong financial situation, you may wish to consider buying a business outright or buying into a business. *Here are two approaches to consider:*

1. Become involved with your chosen going concern as a part-time employee – paid or unpaid
2. Buying an existing business outright and taking total management control

The nature and level of involvement could depend on your skills, experience and degree of financial contribution. This is a stepping stone approach before purchase and you'll get to know the business intimately before you commit, and you will discover the strengths and weaknesses before you invest.

Working within the company before you decide on any further financial commitment will provide on the job experience. What appears to be a healthy profitable organisation on the outside may reveal a different, more sobering reality from the inside.

Due diligence

Before you take any major decisions or make any investment into an ongoing concern, it is important to conduct various aspects of due diligence to establish a number of criteria:

- Who the legal owners are and the shareholding breakdown of the business.
- Looking back over company balance sheets and trading records.
- Checking the current performance - sales, profits, cash flow, outstanding debts, current bank balance etc.

Always seek professional advice from a trusted and recommended source before you enter into any agreement.

The information in this section of the Chapter is purely to act as an aide-memoire and highlight a selection of options that might be possible for you to consider, although there are many more.

Be careful as, whether you are considering buying a business, joining a MLM company, Affiliate marketing, Forex trading or taking on a franchise, there are many unscrupulous people and scams out there! It is advisable, and in your interest, to undertake thorough research on your areas of interest before you commit. You will find that some options will be right for you and some definitely not. This is all about CHOICE!"

Self-Employment – Starting Your Own Business

Self-employment is an attractive alternative as a change of direction. In my experience, it can prove to be even more so if you have previously harboured thoughts of being your own boss, although many people decide to take the leap of faith who have never given self-employment any thought whatsoever. Successful self-employment requires a similar mindset to winning through career change. However, the same rule of thumb applies, i.e. 'one size does not fit all'. Self-employment potentially allows you the flexibility to choose your own hours and to work from home, around family commitments. Of course, it is not always like this, especially when you start out. At the time of writing, around 5 million people were registered as self-employed in the UK. This is the highest figure since records began in 1992, according to the Office for National Statistics (ONS). If you are serious about joining them, you will firstly need to research all of the following and maybe more, depending on what your business does:

- Your business idea
- Your business name
- Your competition
- The most suitable trading structure, e.g. Sole Trader, Partnership or Limited Company
- Business start-up funding/financing your business
- Marketing/business development
- Pricing
- Registering for taxes and National Insurance

- Business premises, i.e. home based, offices etc.
- Your training needs
- Technology requirements
- Developing a business plan

The good news is there is a wealth of information available via the internet from sites such as http://www.startups.co.uk, through various local and regional government agencies, from many of the major high street banks and various regional and national start-up exhibitions. If you decide to set up your own limited company, this is no longer a huge ordeal as you can do so online in a few minutes from around only twenty pounds! Basically you can no longer use 'red tape' as an excuse not to set up. So what is stopping you then? Maybe you?

Every Situation Is Different

Whether self-employment is right for you will depend on what you're looking to achieve and this is where re-evaluation and exploring opportunities are so important. If you decide you want to change career and set up a business of your own, there are many implications to consider. Setting up as self-employed is very simple, but how straightforward your business start-up will be depends totally on the type of business you are planning. An unusual example was a client who decided to set up a very niche style of coffee shop. This is clearly not your everyday type of business, so it needed a huge amount of research, especially around finding the right type of property in the right location, financing, looking at the whole end-to-end process, return on investment etc. It was clear this would take many months of planning, so we needed a contingency. He decided his short term goal was to do other self-employed work, utilising some of the skills we established from his true marketability, from which he could generate income quickly.

This included language tuition and swimming instruction plus some other interests he quickly turned into income streams, while he was developing his 'dream' business. So let's now look at what self-employment or starting a business can offer you, warts and all, as it is not right for everyone.

Weighing Up The Pros And Cons

Let's now consider whether the self-employment pros outweigh the self-employment cons. Not everyone has the same good experience of working from home, working alone, managing staff or running a business, so self-employment or being your own boss isn't suited to everyone. You must weigh up the options to discover your own pros and cons so you can make an informed decision as to whether self-employment or starting a business right for you.

To help your decision making process, the list below is a typical example of some key pros and cons of self-employment. There are no right or wrong answers as you may have completely different views depending on your attitude to these statements. There will also be variances depending on your country of work.

Example table

SELF EMPLOYMENT	
PROs	**CONs**
Be your own boss	You will have to make provision for your own pension and no employer benefits
Reap the rewards of your success	If you are unwell and unable to work you will not earn anything

You do not have to pay income tax until the January following the end of your first year of trading	You will not get paid if you take a holiday
National insurance costs less	You will probably have to work long hours
You can claim tax relief on many items	You will be responsible for any losses
You will have greater freedom than if you were employed	Possible isolation and loneliness (note: collaborations and support networks help overcome this)
No daily commute if you work from home or have premises close to where you live	Constantly marketing and looking for work
Choice – where you work, the work you do, who you work with, how you work, when you work, how you dress	Peaks and troughs of work and income
Working around family commitments	Lack of employer security

If you are excited by the pros of self-employment you have highlighted from this exercise, look at ways in which you can overcome the cons either now or in the medium to long term future. Or do the pros outweigh enough of the cons to make this a viable option for you? Equally do you agree with the pros and cons? If not make up your own list to work through and decide. There is no right or wrong answer but only what feels right for you.

Before you commit to self-employment, if you have a spouse or partner, it is essential to get them on board first. This applies, not just if you set up a company and may need substantial funding, but as a matter of course. Why? Because you are unlikely to be able to guarantee regular income for some while and every business has peaks and troughs, so your income is rarely steady. This is a total change from having a regular salary each month as it requires a very different mindset and careful household financial management.

During troughs you need to ensure that your partner is able provide sufficient financial income to ensure some stability – assuming he or she is working. If your partner isn't working, you must ensure you have enough cash reserves behind you to keep both your business and household going. When the peaks come you have to take full advantage, so it will be all hands to the pump. This could mean working excessively long hours or even 7 full days of the week.

Key developmental activity can be equally demanding on your time and energy but not bring financial rewards for some while. It pays to explain the circumstances to your partner so they can be on board and supportive.

I shared this same thinking with a former neighbour who left a construction company to set up his own building business, soon after buying the house next door to us. The house was in need of major renovation and modernisation to become the family home they desired. However, he was constantly working up to seven days a week on other projects to pay the bills and started to neglect his wife, young family and their home. His wife grew resentful that the essential modernisation of their home was taking a back seat to his other work. He didn't get buy-in from his wife for starting his own business, and he certainly didn't get buy-in for putting his business before the needs of their family and their home. The lack of support from his wife and her frustration at the lack of progress on their own home, eventually drove a wedge between them and sadly impacted on their marriage. Key lesson ...it is essential to get buy-in first!

Businesses Evolve

There is a strongly held view by business gurus that businesses need to constantly reinvent themselves to compete with the changing landscape, demands of new technology and so on. Just as you need to do yourself by changing careers. Therefore if you decide to set up a business don't feel that it will always have to stay the same. The majority of businesses evolve and change over time. Look at Sir Richard Branson. He has spent his career building up businesses, like Virgin Records, selling them then moving into new areas, e.g. Airline, Mobile Phones and Finance. My business bears no relationship today to what it was when I started over 15 years ago. Most businesses will evolve and you will naturally gravitate to the work you enjoy the most, your passions and interests. When I set up my business, word got around and I was suddenly in demand for Reward and Benefits consultancy, which helped to get my business off to a good start. However, I wasn't passionate about this work and although I could command excellent consultancy fees, I was keen to develop my real passions, especially around Career and People Development. As a result, I made sure my Reward and Benefits work became only a small part of my portfolio career and gradually phased it out altogether after a couple of years.

I have continued to refine our business services and products to specialise in aspects of business I enjoy most. Therefore in addition to Career Development, we have kept focus on Executive, Management and Team Development, which all require associate support on projects, as and when needed. My wife is also now a co-director and delivers career and education coaching, working with young people. The key is to keep control of your business focus in line with your passions and key areas of interest, so any changes reflect this. Although some people have major limiting beliefs around the viability of working at your passions, there is a great saying that *"passions build wealth"*.

To this day my business is still evolving, especially with my Steve Preston The Career Catalyst® personal brand, leading Career Coach, Internationally acclaimed Author, speaker and creator of innovative online career and personal development products.

PIT STOP WINNING STEER

Do not, under any circumstances, set up a business exclusively doing something you are good at but don't really enjoy, just because you need to generate income quickly. Although it might work initially it cannot be sustained. This is the same principle as having an employed job you don't enjoy. You won't be fulfilled and people buy people, so your lack of passion will come across to everybody you come into contact with, which is a recipe for disaster!

Mind mapping your decision

If you are someone who likes to use mind maps to brainstorm and collect your thoughts, it can be an excellent way to help you work through your options to decide what job, career or work to do. If you are a very visual person, you might find that mind mapping your options improves the way that you record information, and supports and enhances creative problem solving to aid your decision making process. Within your mind map you can build in options for employment, self-employment or a portfolio career and lifestyle. There are many excellent online mind mapping tools available these days. Some offer 'bells and whistles' but if you want something simple, there are usually free versions which are fine to start you off.

✎ *Exercise – Taking the Leap of Faith*

Now you have had the opportunity to consider some alternative options, to help 'untangle some weeds in your mind', so let's take a look at the Leap of Faith exercise, which will challenge you even further. Carefully think through your answers to the following powerful questions – these have helped many of my clients to achieve sudden 'lightbulb' moments and transform their thinking and their lives! By really being honest and challenging yourself, these key questions will provide you with more clarity and help you make informed decisions to take you to the final Step of the Cycle with greater confidence.

Q1. What would you do if you were not afraid?

Consider your possibilities, what fears you have around these and aim to banish them!

Q2. What would you do if money were no object or all jobs paid the same?

Make a note of whatever comes to mind and do not feel constrained

Q3. What problems can you solve that other people will pay for?

Consider your range of skills and talents you have fleshed out in Step 3 and how you can use some of these to earn income in different ways

Q4. What is stopping you/holding you back?

Consider the barriers/obstacles to achieving your dream and what can you reframe to help you take the leap of faith into new work you love?

Q5. What have you learned from this exercise?

What positive action can you take right now?

How did I take my leap of faith?

This was yet another example of how other people can see things in you that you cannot see for yourself. Having decided I'd had enough of working for other people and wanted to be my own boss, I networked and reconnected with as many people as I possibly could, who I knew had become self-employed and set up their own business. As part of my *exploring opportunities*, I asked them what they had learnt, what they would do differently if they started again and also what they thought I could do in my business and would be good at. I had a few ideas of problems I could solve that people would pay for but nothing concrete.

Everybody was telling me that I had a natural talent for developing people and helping them to achieve their potential. The evidence was staring me in the face but I couldn't see it! Now I had untangled the weeds in my mind, it was much easier to focus on my business offering and the feedback enabled me to develop my original business strap line *'helping you unlock your potential'*. However, it was still scary but as I have stated, you must turn your fear into focus. So, I finally decided to go for it.

Having set my intent, things started happening, as I explained in the introduction. My next leap of faith, was winning my first fee paying work. I remember driving to a meeting with a contact, for some potential Reward and Benefits consultancy, feeling a mixture of excitement, fear and trepidation! I had never done any consultancy work in my life and how on earth was I going to prove I had the knowledge and expertise they required? Maybe you also recognise these limiting beliefs? If so, fear not!

Was what happened remarkable or more likely, just proof, we are our own worst enemies? In the meeting I switched to autopilot immediately, asking key questions, challenging, really getting to grips with the issues the company was facing and making positive suggestions to take the project forward. Suddenly I was told I had exactly the right attitude and approach and was asked "How quickly can you start?"

My emotions driving home were a mixture of euphoria, disbelief, relief and wondering what all the fuss was about! The reality was I had demonstrated my knowledge, expertise, skills and attributes in exactly the same way I would have done in my previous employed role. This winning approach not only allowed me to secure this project, but many others soon followed.

So, why do people make such a song and dance about taking the leap of faith into self-employment? I'm sure you have already worked this out, haven't you? Self-employment or running your own business is similar to winning through career change, as your mindset is key! You are still the same person but you are now working for yourself as opposed to an employer, without your colleagues and other support services you may have relied on. This is just another reframe, as you learnt in Chapter 1. So, what reason are you giving yourself for not using your true marketability in a self-employed role to successfully start up a business of your own? Your answer will determine whether you are now ready to take your own *'leap of faith'*!

Mark's Story (continued)

5

Step 5 – Deciding What To Do

What's IT all about?...

At this point Mark had fully explored the IT Support role but hadn't decided whether to apply for it? Still with some hesitancy he researched a little further, as he didn't fully appreciate the importance that that the company had placed on 'inter-personal skills' above technical IT ability.

He very quickly discovered that having IT capability was all well and good, but in this 'Support' role, which helps employees to use the systems, the company had bad experiences with previous employees who were unable to effectively communicate the best way to resolve problems. Staff operating the systems were often blinded by IT jargon, which caused confusion and lack of trust. Mark's friend was well aware of his excellent verbal communication and inter-personal skills and how these would make a positive difference to his team. With proven ability to quickly adapt and learn new skills, his friend knew he would easily acquire the relevant new IT skills with on the job training.

The combination of my intensive coaching and his friend's endorsement gave Mark the reassurance needed to dispel any remaining fear – instead he was now Feeling Excited And Ready!

Mark began to assess the implications of the new job and put plans in place to mitigate any risks. The new job would pay less than Mark had previously been earning, but the financial evaluation exercise showed that he would still have sufficient money for his outgoings, including that mortgage. Therefore with further coaching on the completion of a compelling job application form, Mark decided to go for it and apply for the job.

But questions remained. Would Mark be shortlisted for interview? Would Mark be confident to undertake IT training to boost his range of skills? Would this job allow him to develop his career further, mindful of the growing importance of IT in any company worldwide? Would he be able to adapt to a new way of working in an office environment with a fixed Monday to Friday format for the first time in his working life?

There's only one way to find out...

...to be continued

- Reassurance is a key part of the Cycle process to build confidence and momentum and cannot be underestimated
- For Mark it was reassurance that provided the impetus to apply for the IT Support role and that this was the right career change for him

Summary

Step 5 - key learning points:

- You do have the CHOICE to reinvent yourself to become the architect of your own future and decide what work you want to do!
- If you are still unclear, imagine you are untangling the weeds in your mind to achieve the CLARITY you want

- It is time to get serious about your 'campaign' as time will fly past and you need to build momentum
- Use the power of The Universal Laws - *'success goes where your energy flows'*
- By changing your mindset around the need to have a JOB, you have multiple choices to decide on the type of work you do next
- Mind mapping your options can help your decision making process
- Understand the pros and cons of self-employment before you jump in headfirst as it isn't for everyone
- Getting additional support from a coach or mentor could make all the difference
- Your mindset and belief will help you transition into self-employment, if this is what you really want

Congratulations, you are now ready to move to the final step of the Career Navigation Cycle - **Taking Positive Action!**

CHAPTER 6

Taking Positive Action – Step 6

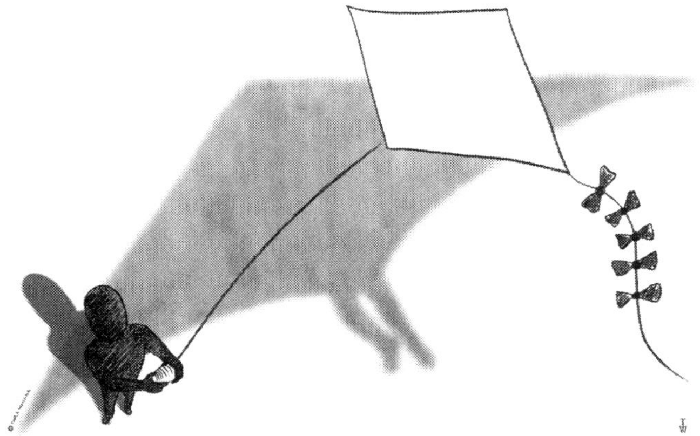

"The same wind blows on us all. It is not the blowing of the wind that determines your destination but the setting of a better sail"

Jim Rohn, Entrepreneur, Author & Motivational Speaker, 1930-2009

Congratulations you have reached the final step of the Cycle and are now well on the way to completing your voyage of self-discovery to achieve a successful outcome. This is where the dawn of reality will definitely kick in, if it hasn't already, as your future can seem exciting or scary or both! The sixth and final step of the process can see you retreat back into your comfort zone, unless you have the right motivation, support and courage. It is about trusting that you have done enough preparation; now you simply need to take a leap of faith to achieve your breakthrough career change.

Just do it

This Chapter could be summed up by a simple matter of the three words made world famous by Nike *"Just Do it!"* Fortunately, I will give you much more practical help than this, to ensure you do have the tools to help you through this final step of the process. However, the Nike slogan is absolutely spot on, as it is **only you** who can ultimately take responsibility to successfully *navigate your way to a brighter future.*

If not now, when will you do what you love?

If you don't follow through on this key final step of the Cycle and transition into doing a job, career or work you love, then when will you? You don't want to be like many people who always talk about doing work they love but are never bold enough to take the action required, do you? I'm sure you don't want to spend the rest of your life thinking 'what if?'

Having taken my leap of faith, over fifteen years ago, I continue to re-evaluate and look at new ways to stretch myself and realise my long term passions and unfulfilled potential, especially my writing and professional speaking. Through writing blogs, articles for trade journals and various personal development websites in the UK and US, this evolved into writing my first book, this book, my *Portfolio Careers* book and I have two other book projects which I aim to complete over the next few years. Therefore, having taken my leap of faith to become a published author, I have become a published author of a series of life changing career and personal development books. The positive publicity has in turn created interest for speaking engagements, seminars and interviews on many radio shows and podcasts, especially in the UK, US and Canada. None of this would have been conceivable in my previous employed career. So I am justly proud of my achievements and especially for continuing to take positive action to make a difference to the lives of others.

Looking back, my love of writing started at school editing the school magazine, writing numerous articles and my first ever career thoughts were of becoming a journalist. I believe we all have latent potential hiding inside us bursting to get out. As already highlighted, if the *WHY* is strong enough, the *WHAT* and *HOW* will follow. It is true that I was encouraged by family, friends, associates and inspiring people I met along the way. People like Leda Sammarco, my book coach, Sue Blake, an amazing publicist, to whom this book is dedicated and most importantly, Ed Peppitt. It was Ed who came to my rescue at a turning point in the publication of my first book, after I had been badly let down by my initial publisher, a leading global brand. Nonetheless, this only spurred me on and served to reiterate the value of continuing to 'take positive action' to make my dream a reality. Above all else, I had to be brave and 'take the leap of faith' to realise my dream. Therefore you, like me, can also reinvent yourself, redesign your career, follow your passions and make them become reality to do work you love!

Follow up and follow through – "Set a better sail"

The secret to this final stage of the Cycle is simple. You must follow up and follow through. You must have the will and desire and commitment to make your successful career transition happen and do so with positive and inspired action.

Get In Shape – Do Some Exercises

Implementing your actions will require clear plans to follow and a certain mental toughness and agility to allow you to persevere and succeed. I am therefore inviting you to enter my 'mind gym' to take some final vigorous exercise. Physical exercise promotes health and wellbeing; mental exercise will create the positive mindset to allow you to take 'positive action'.

✎ *Exercise 1 – Get Fit For Lift Off! The Five Ws check*

With the focus, knowledge and wealth of new insight gained, you should have a much clearer picture of where you are, how you got there and where you are heading, helping you start the all-important process of focused career planning. Imagine you are now on the launch pad ready to blast off into a new and exciting adventure of a fulfilling job, career or work. This book and your new insight is your starter 'tool kit' and you are on countdown to 'lift off'. You can be gripped by the fear of the unknown and hold back and be the 'victim' - never venturing out of your comfort zone. Or you have the opportunity to take control and be the 'architect of your own wonderful future'.

Fasten your seatbelts because the countdown has started and you are on your final checks. It is important to consider and confirm the following status in order to make a smooth take off and a successful landing into your chosen field of work and a brighter future.

WHAT *- Double check your awareness of your 'true marketability' from your life and career. Are you now clear on what you have to offer the world and have identified any learning gaps?*

WHERE *- Your interests, passions and potential fields of activity could be applied, e.g. type of organisation, sector, environment, location or even starting your own business.*

WHO *- Identify your network: the people who can help (eyes, ears, and advocates); the people who can influence, coach, support and steer you in the right direction to unlock the key to your future. It is often the most unlikely people.*

WHEN *- Set a realistic timescale to achieve your successful career change with regular review points. Celebrate small wins along the way that show you are making progress.*

WHY *- Confirm your reasons, values, key motivators/drivers and purpose for your change.*

The Five Ws checks you have just carried out are crucial but wait; one final check has been missed otherwise you could veer off into the abyss!

HOW *- The final check needed to initiate your planning and to implement your strategy with total commitment and belief, not forgetting those all-important contingencies.*

For some people, what holds them back from making a breakthrough change, aside of any fear, is often reframing a few simple aspects around their thinking about the need to have another 'job' and then taking the first steps to make change happen. The following case study will highlight an excellent example of how you can use the *Five Ws* process to challenge your mindset, overcome limiting beliefs, follow your passions and achieve a successful outcome.

Linda's Story – Shifting from 'Job' mindset to a flexible working lifestyle

Linda chose to leave her last job as she no longer felt able to provide the level of support to her client group due to savage cutbacks. Her values had also shifted and she felt at odds with the way the organisation was moving, especially after being overlooked for promotion.

Unfortunately she fell into many of the same traps I have highlighted before. Her conditioning and beliefs were

were based on the need to quickly secure another job. However, she had a fantastic opportunity to re-evaluate and rethink what she wanted from her work and life. Having done so, it became apparent that what she was hoping to achieve would be almost impossible from a typical job, which is why she initially struggled and took some time out. Her priorities were:

Getting some structure – Like lots of busy people, Linda wanted some structure to her days and week. She wanted something each week to look forward to. In exploring opportunities she decided to do some volunteering for a friend who runs a local charity shop. This became such a key part of her life that she now usually adapts her other activities around this key building block.

Choice – Having already turned down a couple of jobs, Linda realised that in returning to work she had the opportunity to focus and create a new framework of work she wanted to do now. This would allow her to follow her passions, play to her strengths, to work with people who valued her and to only work in environments and locations which suited her.

Flexibility – This was one of her most important needs. The reason she turned down some jobs was because of rigid employer expectations. Linda wanted to be the architect of her own future, working on her terms.

This was clearly not a recipe for a typical job! However, once she isolated these key needs and addressed the Five Ws questions she quickly managed to develop what has become a most interesting portfolio career and lifestyle.

In her words:

"My portfolio developed quickly once I had identified what was most important to me. I made the following choices and goals:

1. Give myself the flexibility to work only the days and hours I want
2. Have a variety of work each week
3. Take my holidays when I want to
4. Source, network and identify opportunities which match my values and needs
5. Continue to support and work for my local charity
6. Develop my own private client base, coaching young people to realise their true potential
7. Realise my dream to work with special needs children, primary, infant and nursery school children, which I had long aspired to achieve but thought it too late in my career and life to make this transition
8. Achieve a regular income from doing work I love, which gives me job satisfaction and above all where I feel valued". Having set her intent, Linda achieved all these goals in a matter of months.

Her working week now consists of:

1. A minimum of two days working self-employed in a local school, encompassing a variety of teaching and support roles in the children's centre, primary and junior school
2. Up to one day a week, working voluntarily for a local charity, includes various fundraising events

3. Coaching young people on an ad hoc basis, providing pre and post education support and helping them overcome their barriers to progression
4. Last but not least, co-director of her husband's business, involved with business planning, finances, event management and general support

Linda is another excellent example of a career changer who has proved that, by following the Cycle and taking positive action, you do have CHOICE and it is never too late to do work you love!

✎ *Exercise 2 – Set Sail with the 'Four Cs' Career Action Planner*

Let's now look at the *Four Cs Career Action Planner:* your mission heading for the job, career or work you really want. I have used this simple but highly effective career action planner with hundreds of clients to great effect. I recommend you set this up on a spreadsheet or table, so you can keep adding new actions as you think of them. As with any action plan it is always good practice to add timescales to start and complete different tasks. Don't forget, *'what gets measured gets done!'*

Commence:	Continue:
• Activities you should start now to take positive action and move you towards your end goal	• Activities which are already working for you so you can do more and build momentum
Cease:	**Consider:**
• Activities that are unhelpful, move you away from your goal or any negative mindset that can deter you from achieving your goal	• Any learning gaps and skills required to achieve your goal • The inspiration gained from reading this book, to allow you to make decisions on what to commence or cease in due course

✎ *Exercise 3 – Relax then Stretch*

Moving from your comfort zone into your stretch zone

You don't achieve anything worthwhile in your life without moving out of your comfort zone. So let's do an exercise to help you **give yourself permission** to move out of your comfort zone and take positive action to move yourself forward into the stretch zone. Only by doing this can you take control of your life and career to become the architect of your own future.

There are two parts to this exercise. Consider the diagram below and:

1. Make a note of the words and phrases that apply to how you have seen yourself previously

2. Now consider and write down the words and phrases in the Stretch Zone that relate to how you are now feeling plus those you know you need to work at in order to take positive action.

Complete the comfort zone and stretch zone exercise. Bear in mind that the aim is, the more you take positive action, your comfort zone will shrink and your stretch zone will expand, showing you are achieving real personal growth.

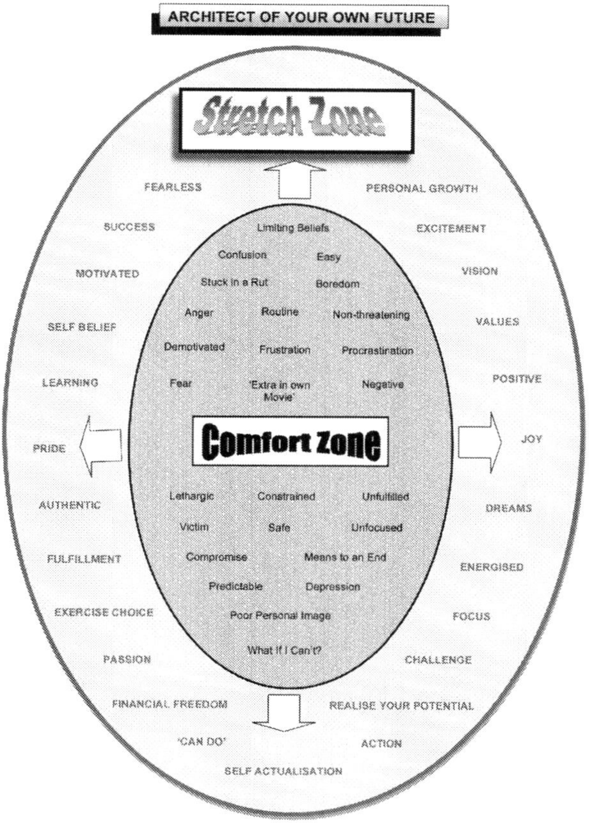

✎ *Exercise 4 – The Eight Key Character Traits to Achieve Successful Change*

Having focused on your action plan, let's now drill down further by looking at another important exercise to stretch you, which requires positive action by you in order to ensure your successful career transition outcome.

These eight key character traits are recognised as making the difference to achieving successful change in your life. Sooner or later you will reach this final step in the Cycle and be ready to *'take positive action'* and you will feel confident in doing so by addressing these eight traits. Some people may resist this final step, but I know that having reached this far you **will** be curious to end on a high note because you will want to achieve your successful career change or transition into a new job, career or work you love.

You have come on a long voyage of self-discovery. Along the way, you will have absorbed a wealth of information and advice. This penultimate exercise is to establish how much you have grown in confidence and are ready to face the challenges ahead. Consider the eight key character traits diagram:

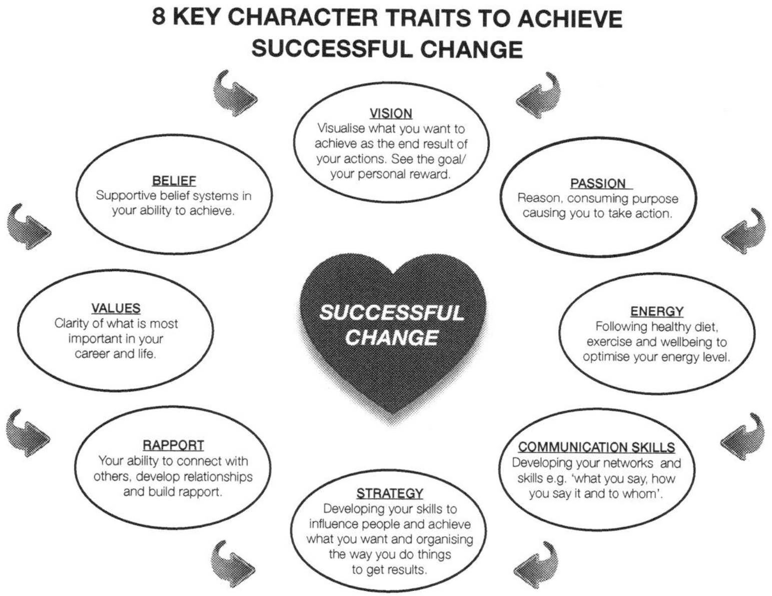

- Take each trait, e.g. Passion, and score yourself out of 10 on how you rate yourself now
- While you are still in transition to your next career step, it is a good strategy to do this exercise at regular intervals so you can review and measure your progress
- Each time you do this exercise, record the date by your scores to allow you to track changes over time
- When you revisit the exercise, it is important not to 'cheat' and look at your previous scores
- To get real benefit, as with all the exercises in this book, you must be totally honest with yourself
- Most importantly, by revisiting some of the exercises in this book, you can focus your energy on maximizing

the traits that are already strong, whilst working even harder on those which need development to build your confidence to the level you want

- Only **you** can now take responsibility for your successful outcome!

The following case study is a wonderful example of a woman who got out of her comfort zone, really stretched herself and took positive action to turn her business idea into a reality.

Helen's Story

Helen came to my breakthrough career change and transition masterclass for two reasons: she was unhappy, not enjoying her job and concerned the impact on own life, outlook, family life with husband young children. She wanted to explore a potential escape route and exit strategy with her Local Authority employer, and work through her options to decide what to do for the best. As a result of coming on the Masterclass, Helen realised she was in absolutely the wrong job for her. She was a classic square peg in a round hole and she couldn't carry on any longer! When exploring her opportunities it became clear that she wanted to take control of her situation and 'become the architect of her own future'. So what did Helen do? She resigned.

Was Helen bold or foolish?

To come to your conclusion, read on but also consider how Helen swiftly moved out of her comfort zone and the impact this had. Another realisation for Helen was an appreciation of all the great skills and attributes she hadn't ever thought about, or just took for granted, as many of us do, don't we? She also had interests and passions, which she could turn into business opportunities. One of these was soft furnishings. Although, at the Masterclass, Helen was totally reluctant to move out of her comfort zone and consider running her own business, when she reflected on the day, she decided that she should not ignore all the evidence. Now was the time, now was the opportunity.

Her voyage of self-discovery on the Masterclass had dramatically boosted her confidence, so she started taking note of what other people were telling her, i.e. maybe she did have what was needed to set up her own business, maybe she could make it work? A few weeks after the Masterclass she took the leap of faith and set up her own soft furnishing business and enrolled on an Open University distance learning degree in soft furnishings. Helen was astounded when immediately she received interest and literally within a few months had an order book which was filled eight months in advance. Absolutely fantastic! Helen sent me a wonderful email explaining all this and thanking me for the insight from the day which had helped transform her career and her life. Most poignantly, her final comment was that her kids had said "We've got mum back", her husband had said "I've got my wife back". But most importantly for Helen… she realised she had got her life back!"

"Freedom lies in being bold"

Robert Frost (American Poet, 1874-1963)

Clearly Helen had been bold and in the process she had achieved her ideal work and life blend. She only worked four days a week, with one day to herself and had become a mum again in the best way possible. It's a wonderful heartwarming story. By investing in my Masterclass and going through the Career Navigation Cycle process on the day, Helen realised how unhappy she really was. Also, by gaining valuable insight from the group, she started to believe in herself, that she did have the skills and talents to run a successful business.

A few years on, Helen took another bold step and set up a partnership with a contact of hers and within a short space of time they were commissioned by none other than Saatchi and Saatchi. What a world of difference and just think how miserable Helen might be now if she hadn't stepped out of her comfort zone and taken some of the bold decisions she had taken over the last few years to secure her freedom.

Learning Points

- Helen went on the same voyage of discovery you have. Like most people, the exercises proved to her she had so much more to offer than she realised, which motivated her to want to change
- Having worked her way round the Cycle and decided what to do, she then took the leap of faith with inspired and positive action to achieve her successful outcome
- If you are or were a square peg in a round hole you can take positive action to change and create the working lifestyle you want
- Remember: "anything is possible, within reason, with the right mindset, belief, skills and positive actions"
- As with all the examples in this book, Helen proved, again, that you should follow your passions and as I have said *'Success goes where your energy flows!"*

This can all be summed up beautifully by Henry David Thoreau's (Poet and Philosopher, 1817-1862) great quote:

"We must walk consciously only part way toward our goals and then leap into the dark to our success!"

✎ *Exercise 5 – Ongoing Plans and Reviews*

So, having completed the exercises so far you need now to take stock. This final exercise encourages you to reflect and review. It will also remind you that the journey never ends and that you continue to learn, grow, develop and flourish. Whichever point you have reached, you should never be complacent, so keep up the momentum and take this opportunity to consider further improvements about what you might want to do next.

How far have I come on my journey?

On the line below plot your position from 1 to 10, where 10 means getting your ideal job or work.

1 2 3 4 5 6 7 8 9 10

Next career transition steps

- How do you move on from where you are today to where you want to be?
- What is the gap made up of? e.g. If you feel you are now at 6 on the scale above, what do you see as the main barriers and key actions to make it to 10 on the scale and to achieve your ideal job, career or working lifestyle?
- Break this down into manageable chunks.

First Career Transition Steps:	Planned Completion Date:	Actual Completion Date:
1.		
2.		
3.		
I will review my progress in these first steps on:		

Outcome of first review:

How good has my progress been? What additional coaching/ support do I need?

Mark's Story (continued)

Step 6 – Taking Positive Action

Sold!

The future suddenly looked a lot brighter as Mark was called to an interview. He was now determined to take positive action to nail the interview. Like most people, Mark wasn't great at selling himself but this was resolved with some focused interview skills coaching to hone his technique and provide compelling answers to likely key questions.

He was now determined to take the final Step and make a successful leap of faith into a new career. The result... Mark got the job and won through to his second major career change in thirteen years. He has since made excellent progress and is enjoying his new career and life again.

...<u>The End</u>... or is this just another beginning?

Once you have got this far just go for it! Consider "what's the worst that can happen?" and put plans in place to mitigate those risks. Many people are known to be quite poor and lack self-confidence when selling themselves at interview, so you are not alone. Your chances of success can be dramatically improved with the right type of professional coaching and support. Yes, this is a commitment of your time and money, but by now, wouldn't you want to invest in a successful future that reaped its own rewards?

Summary

Step 6 Key Learning Points:

- At this final step of the Cycle follow the Nike adage and "Just do it!"
- What have you got to lose by trying something different?
- Take positive action now to avoid thinking 'what if' for the rest of your life
- Work on the Five Ws and Four Cs to shape your direction and 'Set a better sail'
- Cease anything that is not helping you or moving you away from your end goal
- Commence any activities which you need to take positive action on NOW!

- You must move out of your comfort zone and stretch yourself to achieve success
- Build your confidence to make your change by working on the Eight Key Character Traits
- You must change your thinking and beliefs before you can do this!
- If you need structure in your working life, start by finding one thing to build from which you can look forward to each week and you will find your working week will evolve
- It is fine to do work with a mix of paid and unpaid if it works for you – you do have CHOICE!
- You can now review your progress – where you started from, what your successful career change or transition now looks like and the positive action you need to take to achieve this
- It is your future and only you can take responsibility for your successful outcome

Congratulations, you have now completed the six Steps of my Career Navigation Cycle process! I hope you have enjoyed your journey and have been inspired to take action. Please read on for some final thoughts and a fantastic and most inspiring case study so that you, like me and the many people you have read about, can also win through career change and navigate your way to a brighter future!

CONCLUSION

"In the end, it's not the years in your life that count; it's the life in your years!"

Abraham Lincoln (Former US President) 1809 - 1865

This powerful quote from Abraham Lincoln is a fabulous endorsement for my own mantra, which I shared with you in my Introduction and in Chapter 2. Life is too short to be unhappy but rather than looking back on 'wasted' years you may have had, if you can change your thinking and beliefs to this perspective, take the leap of faith and full responsibility for your successful outcome, you cannot go far wrong to achieving happiness and fulfilment in your work and life.

Winning through career change and navigating the career transition maze is a daunting prospect for most people. However, I know that you, like me, may now realise and believe that things usually happen for a reason. Changing career is a fantastic opportunity for you to break out of your comfort zone, take back control of your career and life to do work you really love. You may never get a better chance so take it while you can, as you don't want regrets, do you?

Become The Architect Of Your Own Future

Congratulations, you have completed what I'm sure has been an enlightening voyage of self-discovery! It may have been an emotional roller coaster for you, however, you will know that I have taken great care throughout to demonstrate that my Career Navigation Cycle process works, providing that you follow each step, believe in the process and finally follow through by taking positive action. Reading this book and completing the exercises will have motivated you and have moved you closer to realise the job, career or work you aspire to and create the lifestyle you want. As a consequence, you will now be much better placed to move forward with confidence and belief of what you can do and achieve.

Career Change / Transition Toolkit For Life

Winning through career change and successfully redesigning your career is all about mindset. With the knowledge and insight you have gained from reading this book, you have no reason to ever be 'a square peg in a round hole' and in the wrong job. Likewise, there is no need to be like the majority of people who are unfulfilled in their job or the work they do.

You now have a career change or transition 'Toolkit for Life'. Remember that this is a Cycle, so it is a process that you may go through more than once. Like riding a bike, you may need to hone your skills if you haven't used them for a while but you now have a process and developed skills you can use for the rest of your life.

In order to achieve your successful career change, it is important to plan your onward journey and to review your progress regularly.

Revisiting Your 'Toolkit for Life'

The common thread that has linked every element of my Career Navigation Cycle has been the need to change, especially your thinking. As your confidence has grown and mindset changed you will feel empowered to take that final 'leap of faith' and to fly. The transformation of your thinking is wonderfully encapsulated by The Simplified Law of Cause and Effect. I introduced you to this empowering 'Toolkit for Life' in Chapter 1 and we explored a variety of 'Universal Laws of Success and Achievement in Chapter 5.

When we change our	**THINKING** we change our	**BELIEFS**
When we change our	**BELIEFS** we change our	**EXPECTATIONS**
When we change our	**EXPECTATIONS** we change our	**ATTITUDES**
When we change our	**ATTITUDES** we change our	**FEELINGS**
When we change our	**FEELINGS** we change our	**BEHAVIOUR**
When we change our	**BEHAVIOUR** we change our	**RESULTS**
When we change our	**RESULTS** we change our	**LIFE**

How much have you managed to change your thinking and beliefs, as this is crucial to your success?

If you are still stuck in your comfort zone, I suggest you reread the book or revisit the Chapter where you have got stuck, so you can then move forward with renewed confidence. You may feel now is the time to engage a career coach to help 'untangle the weeds in your mind' to achieve clarity. Finally, remember career change or transition is a process, so you may move back and forth between different steps or go round the Cycle more than once, as it is a virtuous Cycle. No sooner do you get right round than you start again and have to 'let go' of other things to then move forward and start the process again. If this is the case with you, view this as a continuation of your journey, as persistence pays and ultimately you will achieve your desired outcome.

To summarise the learning from this book, I will leave you with the inspiring story of Ruth, a most interesting client who has really embraced the Career Navigation Cycle process to follow and live her remarkable dream.

Ruth's Story

I met Ruth at the Forum 3 Charity exhibition a number of years ago, when I was running seminars on changing careers. Ruth was like many of my clients and other people I have met in various walks of life. She knew she wanted to change careers but had no idea what she wanted to do next or how to go about making her decision – now that might sound familiar to you too? Having attended my seminar and taken on board some of the learning points, Ruth took positive action and put the first stake in the ground by booking on my Breakthrough Career Change and Transition Masterclass. She was young and held a good professional job with a company car. However, Ruth hated her job and wanted to take control of her career and future.

Once she started working her way through the Cycle, it was small wonder she hated her job as she quickly came to realise her job was totally at odds with her values and needs. Her job and the organisational culture was making her desperately unhappy and affecting her whole outlook on life! Ruth's first light bulb moment came on the Masterclass. The group work sparked her into life with new thinking. By the end of the day, she had created her remarkable vision.... lions, Africa, making a difference! Another major light bulb moment was that she had never made a conscious decision about her career in her life. She had let her friends take control of her life by influencing what she studied and where she studied for University, then subsequently even her choice of job and company! It was time to change this and become the architect of her own future doing work she loved and leading a fulfilling life.

The good news is that many of the exercises you have covered in Chapters 1 to 3 really opened up her thinking and have transformed her life. By completing the re-evaluation step, Ruth gained a much clearer understanding of what was important to her in her career and life and WHY? As a consequence she focused on her vision of success and her survival budget. Ruth then made a key commitment to reduce her mortgage payments and use the funding to accelerate the pace of change for her. This really was taking positive action and personal responsibility in a big way! When exploring opportunities, Ruth realised she wanted to live the dream that she had never previously had the opportunity to do.

This set her on a whole new journey to follow her passions, interests and do what she loves with the ultimate goal to work in Africa with 'big cats'. Having completed much research, Ruth took very positive action by studying for an MSc in Wildlife Conservation, learning in her own time, around a full time job. If that's not passion and commitment I don't know what is! She also took the very important step of putting her toe in the water by volunteering at a wildlife park over weekends, a fair distance from where she lives.

This was a big commitment but helped her decide this was definitely the work she wanted to do on a longer term basis. Having followed all six Steps of The Career Navigation Cycle and being totally committed to her goals, Ruth was well on the way to making her dream a reality. She then took even more inspired and positive action by quitting her job, renting out her house and moving to Africa to live the dream! Her career has since taken many twists and turns and she has worked on a number of projects in different parts of Africa, where she has well and truly lived the dream.

Since I started writing this book, she has returned to the UK and is starting on the next phase of her journey, undertaking a PhD. Her research will be investigating children's outdoor environmental experiences for cultivating an authentic connection with nature and the relationship between this connection and developing pro-environmental attitudes and behaviours. This is a far cry from her previous corporate life!

Ruth's inspiring story illustrates perfectly what happens when you take control of your life and your career, unlock your potential and become the architect of your own future! Her approach brilliantly encapsulates all the six Steps of the Cycle, as she has learnt to:

- **Let go and look forward** - break her past conditioning
- **Re-evaluate** – understand what is important to her in her career and life and WHY as her foundation to build from

- **Establish her true marketability** – who she is and what she has to offer the world and boost her confidence and self-belief
- **Explore opportunities** – use volunteering to open up a whole new world for her
- **Decide what to do** – by piecing together the learning from Steps 2-4 and following her passion
- **Take positive action** – by setting her intent, being bold, taking personal responsibility, following through and being true to her values she has truly become the architect of her own future!

Navigate Your Way To A Brighter Future

Just as I achieved my breakthrough career change over a decade ago, so can you. The many inspirational examples I have shared with you in this book have also achieved their breakthroughs or are well on the way to doing so and illustrate without doubt that it is possible. My aim is to equip and inspire you to become the architect of your own future, to win through career change and successfully redesign your career, doing work you love.

Some final thoughts:

- Remember success is about the journey, so recognise your achievement in completing the Career Navigation Cycle process as a major step towards relaunching your career
- Continue developing your networks, embracing Social Media and being opportunistic
- Whatever you set out to do now is likely to evolve and change - you now have a toolkit to help achieve your vision of success now and for the future

- The key to unlocking your potential is self-awareness – continue to grow personally as well as professionally to become the best person you can be
- Learn more and you will earn more!
- If you have found it difficult to make your transition on your own, seek expert help sooner rather than later, utilising the knowledge you have gained from this book

I have also provided many additional resources, including bonus extras not featured in the book, on my website. These tools are to help you work towards achieving your successful career change.

The toolkit contains:

- Free electronic worksheets for many of the key exercises in the book
- Free MP3 download -The first 30 minutes of my 'I Want A Career Change' 4CD/MP3 audio book set
- Free downloadable PDF with 5 pages of my Top Career Change Tips

You can download this toolkit of resources by registering at: **http://www.steveprestonthecareercatalyst.com**

Having reached this point, people often feel that they have enjoyed their voyage of self-discovery and so I wish you well with your quest. As you are now coming to the end and have almost finished reading, you may already start to have some good ideas. Whatever your current position may be, you will have learnt loads about yourself from the processes in this book keeping in mind the opportunity to further develop your career and aspirations from my future books and coaching programmes. By now, you will have some excellent tools for life, an understanding of the power of a positive mindset and be less fearful of change knowing that my six Step Career Navigation Cycle will help you to find fulfilment in your work and life. What could be better than this?

I wonder if you realise yet, just how far you have come and how much you have truly learnt? I would love to hear from you via my website **http://www.steveprestonthecareercatalyst.com** where you can sign up now to receive my blog and newsletters.

I would value your review

Now you have completed the book, in order to spread the word about *'Winning Through Career Change'*, I would be most grateful for and value your honest review on Amazon.

If you have already become the architect of your own future and achieved your desired goal as a result of reading this book, many congratulations! It is great if you have now found a career or work that you love and achieve fulfilment to follow in the footsteps of the many inspiring examples in the book.

As you read this last page you will begin to truly understand the value of my Career Navigation Cycle and that you can win through career change and navigate your way to a brighter future. There is nothing to be gained by standing in the shadows, is there? 'Just Do It' and have belief in yourself, as I have now given you the tools to pursue change and follow new opportunities. Just like me, and the inspiring examples in this book, you will now appreciate the importance of taking that final Leap of Faith. If you follow through with the learning from this book, consider how it would feel to soar like an eagle and into a new era of your life? After you have read this final poem... just relax, close your eyes, visualise your journey so far and you now achieving a successful outcome!

'Come to the edge.'

'We can't. We're afraid.'

'Come to the edge.'

'We can't. We will fall!'

'Come to the edge.'

And they came.

And he pushed them.

And they flew.

Guillaume Apollinaire,
Poet, Playwright and Novelist, 1880-1918

STEVE'S

Inspirational Career & Personal Development Resources

Steve has created a toolkit of additional resources for you, including many bonus extras not featured in the book. These tools are to help you work towards achieving a successful career change, regardless of your situation.

The toolkit contains:

- Free electronic worksheets for many of the key exercises in the book
- Free MP3 download -The first 30 minutes of Steve's highly acclaimed *'I Want A Career Change'* 4CD/MP3 audio book set
- Free downloadable PDF with 5 pages of Top Career Change Tips to help your career change quest, including a link to Steve's special online Career Values and Needs Tool - use code **CVN10** to save £10!

You can download this toolkit of resources by registering at: **http://www.steveprestonthecareercatalyst.com**

In addition, Steve has a wide range of Career and Personal Development books, online products and coaching services to support your journey in *'winning through career change'* and navigating your way to a brighter future:

Career Change

Innovative and Inspirational Online Career Change & Transition Programme - *Navigate Your Way To A Brighter Future* – *6 steps to transform your career and life*

Available at: **http://www.steveprestonthecareercatalyst.com/online-career-change-programme/**

Breakthrough Career Coaching with Steve –
Programmes for professionals and executives
Available at: **http://www.steveprestonthecareercatalyst.com/career-coaching/**

Career Values & Needs Exercise Tool

SPECIAL READER OFFER:
Save £10 using code CVN10

Available at: **http://www.steveprestonthecareercatalyst.com/product/career-values/**

Audio book 4 MP3/CD set – *I Want A Career Change* –
6 steps to navigate the way to a brighter future
Available at: **http://www.steveprestonthecareercatalyst.com/product/i-want-a-career-change-mp3-audio-book/**

Book – *Winning Through Career Change* – Six steps to navigate your way to a brighter future *(Kindle version)*
Available at: **http://www.steveprestonthecareercatalyst.com/winning-through-career-change/**

Portfolio Careers & Lifestyle

Book – ***Portfolio Careers - How To Work for Passion, Pleasure & Profit!*** *(Kindle and paperback)*

Portfolio Career Masterclass – ***How to Work for Passion, Pleasure & Profit!***

Both available at:
http://www.stevepreston thecareercatalyst. com/ portfolio-careers/

Breakthrough Career Coaching with Steve –
Programmes for professionals and executives
Available at: **http://www.stevepreston thecareercatalyst. com/career-coaching**

Audio book 2 MP3/CD set – ***How Colourful is your umbrella***
Create a working life where you will enjoy Mondays as much as Fridays!
Available at: **http://www.stevepreston thecareercatalyst. com/product/how-colourful-is-your-umbrella-mp3- audio-book/**

Redundancy

Book – ***Winning Through Redundancy*** – Six steps to navigate your way to a brighter future *(Kindle and paperback)*
Available at: **http://www.stevepreston thecareercatalyst. com/about-steve-preston-the-career-catalyst/winning- through-redundancy/**

Breakthrough Career Coaching with Steve –
Programmes for professionals and executives
Available at: **http://www.stevepreston thecareercatalyst. com/career-coaching**

ABOUT

Steve Preston

Recognised as 'The Career Catalyst'®, Steve has transformed the lives and careers of thousands of people from many business sectors and walks of life. An internationally acclaimed author, speaker and leading career coach, Steve is passionate about helping unlock and fulfil people's potential. He especially enjoys helping people change careers and achieve the working lifestyle of their choice.

Steve thrives on sharing his knowledge and experience to challenge your thinking about the world of work and what work you can do. He inspires people to follow your passions, do work you love and lead a fulfilling life. Steve runs breakthrough career development coaching programmes for professionals and executives and periodically unique Portfolio Career Masterclasses. He also has developed a highly acclaimed innovative online career change & transition programme and a wide range of inspirational career and personal development books and audio books.

Steve is a prolific writer, having written numerous articles for blogs, trade journals, career and personal development websites in the UK, US, Australia, New Zealand and LinkedIn

Pulse. Steve is also a keynote motivational speaker at high profile career events, conferences and professional associations and has been featured around the globe in media interviews, radio shows and podcasts.

A key part of Steve's portfolio career is also as MD and Owner of specialist consultancy, SMP Solutions (Career & People Development) Ltd, providing quality outplacement, career transition and people development programmes, especially for organisations undergoing key change.

How to book or connect with Steve

If you would like to engage Steve to speak at your event, coach or mentor you, sign up for his blogs, learn more about his many products and services or just become part of his online communities, please contact or follow him by any of the following means...

Email: **steve@steveprestonthecareercatalyst.com**

Website: **www.steveprestonthecareercatalyst.com**

Facebook:
https://www.facebook.com/TheCareerCatalyst

Twitter:
https://twitter.com/stevempreston

LinkedIn:
http://www.linkedin.com/in/steveprestonsmpsolutions

SMP Solutions (Career & People Development) Ltd:
www.smp-solutions.co.uk

YouTube Channel:
https://www.youtube.com/channel/UCj0dyVi9gborbV0fLSZ7iow?view_as=public

ABOUT
Tara Winona

Art and words woven together, capturing the power of life changing moments...

Tara Winona creates images with the desire to tell stories. Often with double meanings, Tara's art seeks to celebrate the power of the imagination and capture the magic of life changing moments, motivated by an innate desire to see us all reach our potential. Her inspiration comes from her life adventures, a love of storytelling and an endless fascination with nature.

Originally Tara trained as a designer and illustrator in Australia. Then, for many years, she created and directed spectacular international events by painting with lasers, lights, fireworks and sound. She has lived in Milan, Paris and London, travelled the world several times, became two languages wiser and is now able to say 'thank you' in at least 30 different countries. She has had a lot of crazy adventures, some of them particularly hair-raising, which she might write a book about one of these days...

One day, Tara took a leap of faith and rented an art studio. She began to create just for herself. A wonderful fulfilling love affair was rekindled and thus Tara began to 'follow her star'.

Steve and Tara met when she was showing her 'Reach for Your Dreams' paintings - a series which show a little red headed girl taking leaps of faith and learning to be courageous. Steve 'got it' and an instant friendship was formed. They talked about Steve writing a book and Tara doing the illustrations and, one day, Steve took his own leap of faith. As Steve says, *"life is too short to not do what you love!"*

Steve has helped Tara to her win through her own career change. She has truly arrived, most notably to have now become a successful, internationally exhibited artist!

Tara and her husband are also now truly living their dream, sharing their time living and working between London and Sydney.

www.tarawinona.com

24027022R00181

Printed in Great Britain
by Amazon